The PUNCH
BOOK OF CRIME

Edited by
ALAN COREN

A Punch book published by Punch Publications Limited
In association with Robson Books Limited

Printed in Great Britain by Leagrave Press
ISBN 0 903895 95 I

Distributed by Robson Books Ltd, 28 Poland Street, London W1V 3DB

CONTENTS

FOREWORD

YOU will hear much snorting and twittering in those manicured banlieues where the well-heeled hang their bowlers about the fact that in 1976 the prison population of this country reached a record 42,000, and that the upkeep of same, at £3,870 per lag per annum, was also a record. Why, cried those on the outside, should Honest Decent Folk (and here the HDF whipped out their shiny pocket computers to calculate that each of them paid £4 a year to keep his less fortunate fellows clinked) have to cough up so much hard-earned coin?

There are many answers, practical, political, moral, metaphysical, and daft; but there is one answer which leaves all others at the post, and that is that we on the outside owe much to those on the inside, and that if some bleak maximum security vault fancies a bit of chintz curtaining or a colour telly, we should not begrudge it. Because there is one villain to every thousand beyond the walls, and he is doing porridge for the rest of us. There, but for the grace of an inordinate number of factors, go we.

Or, rather, stay we.

For most of us are, at some time, villains; and saved from penalty only by circumstances. The honest decent citizen who takes his girlfriend out to lunch and claims the bill on expenses, pockets an office biro on his way home, drinks four large scotches and gets behind his steering-wheel, and, arriving at Dunromin, pokes his wife on the snoot, has been guilty of enough offences to get him sent down without the option. Only by luck, habit, tradition, does the souvenir ashtray, the excess insurance claim, the smuggled brandy, the fiddled tax return, the unlicensed chihuahua, not end up on the Clerk's table with *Exhibit A* gummed to it.

This anthology, then, does not concern itself solely with the crimes of professionals; you do not need to have pulled a stocking over your face or filleted a cathedral roof in the small hours to find yourself somewhere in these pages. Nor, I hope, should the seriousness of crime prevent us from appreciating its comedy; for the criminal element is a human element and is by definition, therefore, a comic element. And the criminal is just like the rest of us, only worse; but, then, don't we perhaps feel that about everybody?

ALAN COREN

Who was that Lady?

If Patty Hearst's defence that her personality was completely changed by brainwashing is accepted, KEITH WATERHOUSE foresees some confusion in the English courts

"PRISONER at the bar, are you Alfred Montmorency Cuthbertson, of No. 14 Clement Attlee Boulevard, in the Borough of Smokeville?"

"No, sir. I am James O'Flaherty Nairns, of the same address."

"According to the indictment you are Alfred Montmorency Cuthbertson. Have you at any time so styled yourself?"

"Yes, sir. I was Alfred Montmorency Cuthbertson on August the nineteenth of last year."

"And only on that day?"

"Yes, sir."

"And before that you were James O'Flaherty Nairns?"

"No, sir. Before that I was Terence Craven Wilkes, importer of dried fruits. On August nineteenth of last year I became Alfred Montmorency Cuthbertson, unemployed sexual fetishist. I resumed my identity as Wilkes shortly after my arrest. After my first remand in the lower court I became James O'Flaherty Nairns, a free-lance billiard-table renovator, distance no object."

"Then you are James O'Flaherty Nairns?"

"Yes, sir. That is my name."

"James O'Flaherty Nairns, you are charged with that on the nineteenth of August 1975 you did steal or feloniously take away five pairs of transparent knickers, the property of one Alice Clara Butterworth or Beatrice May Trelawney. How do you plead, guilty or not guilty?"

"Not guilty."

"One moment, Mr Bracegirdle. Do you intend to call many more witnesses?"

"Several, m'lud."

"Then perhaps you will be good enough to set my and the jury's mind at rest on the rightful ownership of these knickers. Did they belong to

Mrs Butterworth or Miss Trelawney?"

"To both, m'lud."

"They shared their knickers?"

"They are one and the same person, m'lud. If I may crave your lordship's indulgence: it will be part of the prosecution's case that shortly before this offence was committed, or alleged to have been committed, Terence Craven Wilkes was lodging at the home of Alice Clara Butterworth, a widow and part-time lollipop lady. You will hear the prisoner Nairns claim that as Wilkes he was brainwashed into becoming Alfred Montmorency Cuthbertson. It was as Cuthbertson, the prosecution contends, that he in turn brainwashed Mrs Butterworth into becoming Beatrice May Trelawney, a film extra."

"How did he achieve that?"

"By telling her repeatedly that he could get her into show business, m'lud."

"And did he?"

"No, m'lud, because later that day he stole her knickers and removed himself to the Great Northern Hotel where he booked a room under the alias of Nicholas Johnstone Willoughby."

"Then at the time the articles were stolen, Mrs Butterworth was in effect Miss Trelawney?"

"Yes, m'lud."

"Would it not assist the jury if you were to call her Miss Trelawney?"

"No, m'lud, because she has since resumed the identity of Mrs Butterworth and it will be under that name that she will later be giving evidence."

"Very well, Mr Bracegirdle. Let us get on."

* * *

"Mr Nairns, you have heard Inspector Ffinch say that he interviewed you at the Great Northern Hotel and after some conversation you showed him five pairs of knickers. Is that true or not?"

"It is not true. Alfred Montmorency Cuthbertson showed the knickers to Detective-sergeant Gryce."

"How do you know, Mr Nairns?"

"Because I was there."

"You were, at that time, Alfred Montmorency Cuthbertson?"

"Yes, although I was using the name of Nicholas Johnstone Willoughby in order to confuse Detective-sergeant Gryce."

"Who is Detective-sergeant Gryce?"

"He is the man who has just given evidence under the name of Inspector Ffinch."

* * *

"I am sorry to recall you to the witness box, Inspector. Is your real name Detective-sergeant Gryce?"

"I was Detective-sergeant Gryce, sir. The accused brainwashed me into becoming Inspector Ffinch."

"And you are still Inspector Ffinch?"

"I am, sir."

"It is a trifle odd, is it not, Inspector, that after undergoing a complete change of personality to the extent that you have a new name, you should still remain a policeman?"

"I am not a policeman, sir. I am a bus inspector."

* * *

"To resume your evidence, Mr Nairns. You do not contest that these knickers were stolen, or that they were stolen by Alfred Montmorency Cuthbertson?"

"No, sir."

"Or that you yourself were, at the relevant time, the same Alfred Montmorency Cuthbertson? That is common ground, is it not?"

"It is."

"And it is your defence to this charge that you have undergone a change of personality—indeed, two changes of personality—and that as James O'Flaherty Nairns you are not responsible for the crimes of Alfred Montmorency Cuthbertson."

"That is so, sir."

"Now by your own admission, Mr Nairns, when you were arrested as Alfred Montmorency Cuthbertson by Inspector Ffinch, now known to be Sergeant Gryce, you were using the alias of Nicholas Johnstone Willoughby so as to escape arrest. How do we know that the name of James O'Flaherty Nairns is not likewise an alias, and for the same purpose of evading the penalty of the law?"

"It is not an alias, sir. I am Nairns."

"How do you *know* you are Nairns?"

"I have a moustache."

"Didn't you have a moustache when you were Terence Craven Wilkes?"

"Yes, but I shaved if off when I became Alfred Montmorency Cuthbertson."

"And now you have grown it again?"

"Not the same one."

"Mr Nairns, will you tell the court how, as Terence Craven Wilkes, you became Alfred Montmorency Cuthbertson?"

"Yes, sir. As Terence Craven Wilkes I quietly imported dried fruits and was normal in every way except for a repressed desire to dress up in women's clothes and accost sailors. One evening I was introduced to a social club where I met the Clerk of the Court."

"But he was not the Clerk of the Court then, was he, Mr Nairns?"

"No, sir. He didn't become Clerk of the Court until he met Inspector Ffinch down at the bus depot. At that time he was a drag artist."

"And he persuaded you to put on lipstick and become Alfred Montmorency Cuthbertson?"

"He was very persuasive."

"Go on, Mr Nairns."

"As Cuthbertson, sexual deviate and knicker-thief, I was deeply ashamed and could only live with myself by becoming Wilkes again. But, having had a taste of being Cuthbertson, I found life as Wilkes very dull and boring. While on remand I met a warder named David Peregrine Hargreaves and we got talking. He persuaded me to become James O'Flaherty Nairns, free-lance billiard-table renovator, and I in my gratitude persuaded him to become Henry Lovelace Bracegirdle, barrister-at-law."

"But *I* am Henry Lovelace Bracegirdle, Mr Nairns."

"Exactly, sir. It's a small world, isn't it?"

* * *

"Before commencing the case for the defence, m'lud, may I ask for your lordship's guidance on a matter that has been troubling me? It revolves on the question of whether I am still qualified to advise my client."

"What is the matter, Mr Copperdale?"

"With your lordship's permission, that's just it—I am Mr Copperdale no longer. During the luncheon recess I was brain-washed by my client and am now a TV impressionist named Ron Bingley, the man of a thousand voices."

"Don't be absurd, Mr Copperdale."

"Absurd, my lord? You dirty rat! Play it again, Sam. And who's this coming into court now? It's no other than Tommy Cooper. Just like that."

* * *

"James O'Flaherty Nairns or whatever your name is, pay attention to me. The jury have found you guilty, and rightly so in my opinion of a mean and despicable offence. Society has to be protected against animals like you and were I still a Crown Court judge I would think five years a not excessive sentence. However, since having a discussion in my chambers with Mr Ron Bingley, the man of a thousand voices, on a point of law, I have become Terence Craven Wilkes, importer of dried fruits and repressed transvestite. Before you leave the dock a free man, Nairns, I will trouble you for the name of that drag club you used to go to."

"Tut-tut! Pause for a laugh there!"

SO MUCH TIME, SO LITTLE SPACE

Inside Britain's crowded jails with HONEYSETT

"This is nothing—you should see it at meal-times."

"Try Wormwood Scrubs."

". . . nineteen, twenty. Right, now we'll imagine twenty press-ups."

"Was there anything else, apart from wanting to sit down for a bit?"

"You've been acting very strangely since you came out, Sid."

We have Alan Coren
Is there any advance on 4 quid?

THE ear may be a dust trap, but when it comes to keeping your sunglasses on, it has clear advantages over a drawing-pin pressed into the side of your head.

These days, we must concern ourselves over such details.

Similarly, there are many places for a forefinger, and a matchbox isn't one of them. Decimalisation is tricky enough, without our having to convert imperial pints on an arsenal of only nine digits.

Anyone currently awash in my drift has clearly not been reading the newspapers: kidnapping, it seems, has much in common with rabies in that, having swept the European mainland in the last few years, it now stands poised at Calais waiting for a good following wind, and if Something Is Not Done the people of Britain may well, in the days to come, find themselves spending more and more time in car-boots, tea-chests, cellars and attics while their loved ones scurry back and forth in frantic attempts to drum up something negotiable to wrap in brown paper and leave in a hollow tree off the A41.

I give you, courtesy of the *Daily Express,* Mr Peter Heims, editor of *Top Security.* As if it weren't disturbing enough to think that there's enough interest in the subject to merit a magazine called *Top Security*, its editor has a tale to make thy two eyes, like stars, start from their spheres: for he is presently gumming together a seminar at a Heathrow hotel to discuss ways in which potential British kidnappees can keep the stocking-mask from the door, and those invited include such top retailers as Marcus Sieff, John Sainsbury and Sir John Cohen (which just goes to prove that there is a darker side to turning over umpteen million jars of jam than lying on one's yacht and totting up the week's gross), plus *fifteen hundred* others, like Richard Burton, who have made no secret of the fact that they have no need to duck into a doorway when they spot their bank-manager strolling towards them.

Addressing this throng of collateral will be a team of experts including Sir Geoffrey Jackson, our erstwhile ambassador in Uruguay, who was recently nicked by Tupamaros, and who avers: "We must bring home to people that kidnapping can happen here and that it's got to be stopped. It is important to step up manpower and firepower in making it infernally difficult to be captured." He then, having got the blood racing and Messrs. Smith and Wesson excitedly scribbling quick calculations on the back of an old cartridge-box, adds an even more disquieting coda: "But if terrorists really want to get you, believe me they will."

And it is that small phrase which sends the brain spinning into crazed speculation: "if terrorists really want to get you". For how does one determine that, fathom the convoluted, possibly illogical, workings of the terroristic psyche? Might they want to get *me*? Or would it be mere money up the spout to bung an electrified fence around the premises, mount a Bofors gun on the roof, chain myself to the boiler, and invest in a matched pair of Dobermanns of such keyed-up suspiciousness that they would be as likely to start stropping their fangs on the master's shins as go for the putative kidnapper?

On the surface, yes. The tie that binds such unlikely bedfellows as Mr Burton and Sir John Cohen is their common ability to spill noughts on a cheque without a second thought, and needless to say I am not of their number. The number I am of is £137·63, at the last count, and I'm not altogether certain it didn't have a red "O" against it, come to think; and one of the few things I feel entitled to guess about kidnappers is that they do not go to all the trouble of grabbing a customer only to find themselves with an overdraft to pay off. One's first thought, indeed, is that it's rather comforting to know (since I haven't been invited to attend) that there are fifteen hundred blokes standing between oneself and the Elastoplast gag, and that British kidnapping will have to become something of a craze before the threat gets around to me.

One's second thought, however, is that the said fifteen hundred would be pretty dumb to stand up and be counted, that what Mr Heims has probably got on his hands is a vast empty auditorium with Sir Geoffrey Jackson staring down at it, and that Britain's would-be kidnappers are back to square one, i.e. pot luck.

So what? you say. Even if they're not going to be ticked off that Heathrow guest-list, there are still large stocks of millionaires around, all of them better quarry than a bloke with nothing more than £137·63 of someone else's money. True enough; but there's scant consolation there, because a quite unsettling aspect intervenes in the argument at this point.

As you doubtless know, Italy, is so beset with kidnappings these days that it is virtually impossible to drive through Rome or Milan for the vast traffic-jams of plain vans containing solvent citizens trussed like chickens. As a result of this, rich men have taken to dissembling: they drive battered old Fiats, wear crumpled off-the-peg suits, sport tin watches, smoke dog-ends, and, more ominous than any of this, actually pay a new breed of PR men to spread the word in the public prints that they are on their uppers and do not know where their next lira is coming from. It's reaching the point where, unless these terrified lads are very lucky indeed, they will be snatched *for looking so broke they could only be loaded!*

It is therefore open season on everybody. And, if Sir Geoffrey's any judge, the same could happen here: merely by drawing attention to my overdraft I ensure that kidnappers immediately assume me to be drowning in the stuff. Ah, you say, but when they find out, they'll let you go!

Yes, I reply, and probably in slices.

Then again (and here we wade into yet murkier depths), though I may personally be broke, that is not to say there are not people on whom my kidnappers might lean, assuming *them* to have the wherewithal to repurchase me. So I have to begin asking all sorts of questions I would prefer to leave unframed, e.g. how much would *Punch* pay to get me back? A thousand? Fifty thousand? Anything? True, there might be some goodwill to be gleaned from forking out a few bob to save a loyal colleague, but Wm. Wordsworth is not the only hack to hear Two Voices: I hear another saying, with maximum TV coverage, "Much as we love Mr Coren, we feel that a stand must be taken NOW if the country is not to be overtaken by a wave of similar atrocities. Let us stand up to these thugs! Let them see that we would rather sacrifice one man than put a thousand in jeopardy! This magazine has always stood for law and order, for decency and courage, for an Englishman's right to walk the streets without fear, for rattling good value at only 25p and although in this week's bumper issue there is no article by Mr Coren, there are nevertheless pages and pages of wonderful hilarious . . . "

The kidnappers might send the note to my wife, of course, and I've no doubt she could scrape a few bob together, here and there, under the circumstances, and certainly would. Almost certainly would. It has just occurred to me that due to that quirk of fate that men call insurance policies, I am worth a considerable amount of negotiable tender, dead. Normally, this would not weigh at all with this warm and devoted girl;

but let us just suppose that I was snatched on a day upon which we had been bunging saucepans at one another and . . .

She would, of course, change her mind when the heat died down, but by then, if I happen to fall into impatient hands, I could well be anchored in the Estuary by a pair of concrete socks and moving only with the assistance of the tide.

I am not sure what to do for the best. Like most of us, I have up until now reckoned my redemption to be in hands about which I could do nothing. Human beings, I fear, are fallible redeemers. I suppose the only course is to remove the uneasy options from them, and see to it that one isn't nicked in the first place.

I intend to have THIS BELONGS TO THE MAFIA tattooed on my chest. It may be painful, but it'll hurt less than having an ear removed at the root, and will almost certainly prevent it.

Provided, that is, I get a kidnapper who can read.

INSIDE BRITAIN'S JAILS

Soft or hard cell? State-supported Hiltons, or dumps where you wouldn't keep a dog? Reforming holiday camps, or breeding grounds for trainee criminals? Too much telly, or legalised brutality? We offered insider RICHARD NEVILLE the chance to grass.

WITHIN twenty minutes of my first spell in the exercise yard at Her Majesty's prison, Wormwood Scrubs, I was let into a secret of Scotland Yard's department of dirty tricks. The secret was revealed to me in detail by a fellow prisoner, as we plodded around the walled enclosure, a lugubrious crocodile in the afternoon drizzle. From this man I learnt that finger-prints had legs. That a set of prints could easily be removed from, say, an ashtray and then wrapped convincingly around the handle of a gun.

It's all done with Sellotape.

This prisoner insisted that he himself had been convicted by his own print, so transported, and that he wasn't the only one. (*The moving finger prints, and having printed, is moved on.*) It took at least five years for this forensic dynamite to explode in the witness box at the Old Bailey, when in 1975 a Scotland Yard alchemist finally broke down under cross examination and admitted that, yes, finger-prints *could* be moved. Lawyers seemed perturbed and senior police officers must have shuffled papers with a faint air of embarrassment. It was widely noted that the days were over of the damning inviolability of such evidence. It was the end of a time honoured tradition, but no-one was let out of gaol.

The point to remember is this: when it comes to criminology, the exercise yard at the Scrubs is several years ahead of the rest of the world. You can pick up all sorts of tricks at these universities of crime. By the end of the first week a receptive inmate receives a thorough grounding in the finer points of burglary, gas meter cracking and how to sell (occupied) stately homes to Americans by mail order. At times I was reminded of a couplet from the old school song—so much more appropriate for Her Majesty's institutions of correction than it ever was for the quadrangles of outer Sydney:

Do not think that we'll forget
Lessons that we treasure yet.

Six years since I was sprung, and still I haven't forgotten how to scratch out the vault plan of a certain bank on the back of a biscuit. (Any offers?)

The atmosphere of British gaols is reminiscent of some British hotels, inasmuch as the staff dutifully set out to make your stay as miserable as possible. By some mysterious code of correction known only to the Home Office, the inmate is subjected to a waking life of rigid regimentation and a constant climate of verbal bullying and abuse. The road to rehabilitation must be paved with humiliation. Although it should be made clear that not *everyone* you meet in a uniform, from the first moment of apprehension to the last farewell at the prison gates, is a bastard. But since when did the nice ones ever end up giving the orders?

For many, it's twenty-three hours a day in a one-man cell with two other inmates. The other hour is spent in the exercise yard, invariably surrounded by uniformed screws barking fitfully. It gets to be a little humdrum—even after ten days, which is so far my longest stretch. Not that prison is without its moments of untrammelled relief. On Sundays, there is chapel service. It's one parish where there is no decline in attendances. Heartening, perhaps, for Archbishops, who should remember that the rival attraction is one more hour in the cell.

Even so, there is not much to choose between the two. Chapel in a bigger cell with more people, where the iron bars are not made of stained glass. Still, it's another chance to talk to prisoners. Or rather, sing. In gaols where the free association of inmates is forbidden, as at Wandsworth when I was there, hymn time is when the captive congregation converses in musical cadences which pose as words from the verses; a free-form singalong.

On Sunday evening one looks forward to the film show which soon becomes group therapy, as everyone joins in cheering the baddies and booing the police. For the other six days, it's back in the cell.

The monotony of living three in a room, day after day, drives most men to accept the only alternative: work. Do not assume the Home Office is unimaginative in its supply of occupations available or that prisoners spend all day sewing mailbags. In some gaols, inmates can be assigned either to books, imprinting number plates or spending all day sewing mailbags.

It is considered part of the process of rehabilitation for the prisoner to be gainfully employed. Although not *too* gainfully. It is not considered part of the process of rehabilitation for the prisoner to be paid a wage—merely some derisory sum of pocket money.

Believing that incarceration itself be punishment enough and without wishing to have added to it the languors of slavery, I applied to the Governor for permission to possess a typewriter (dimly recalling that Bertrand Russell, in the days when extra facilities could be rented, dashed off an immortal tome in an atmosphere of tablecloths and champagne).

"Of course you can't have a typewriter," snapped the Governor, ordering me from the office with irritation. The reason, as it later transpired, was thought to be obvious. The authorities were afraid that the machine would be used by the prisoner to attempt a further offence while in custody, to wit, commit suicide. It was a touching realisation. How could they have known that I secretly planned to splice my tongue in the roller and tap myself to death with the askerisk?

It would be seen as such a waste of a typewriter and, after all, the official methods are more refined. Food for instance, an enforced suicide by instalments. I'll never forget my welcome to the cuisine of Brixton. It was the first meal after 24 hours of being buffeted about in a Black Maria and hanging around the grimy basements of courtrooms. A saucer full of tinned spaghetti rings, cruelly cold. By the time it arrives, you're so hungry you go ahead and vomit it up anyway. To be fair, it is not always so challenging. There's ample starch-enriched bread to fill up the holes. To *clog* up the holes. It would be unseemingly to dwell in these august pages on the problems of adjusting one's rectal habits to the exigencies of Her Majesty's prison routines. Let's just say that it severely slackens morale. I tried to console myself with the advice Paul Getty allegedly dishes out to his nephews after a meal at a sumptuous restaurant. So as not to waste valuable elements of nutrition, "Hold it in as long as possible." It seemed I was involuntarily sharing the bowel-style of the super rich.

Fantasies of sitting pensively in a cell to create continued, and so I applied for writing material, which later arrived. A pencil with an official exercise book in which I set out to chronicle my decline and fall. There was only one catch. On the cover of the book was an imposing list of regulations governing its use—the breach of any of which rendered the contents liable to immediate confiscation and destruction. From memory, this is its drift:

"The prisoner is forbidden to write about the following:

1. His own life.
2. The life in this institution of correction.
3. The life in any institution of correction.
4. The circumstances of the prisoner's crime.
5. Or court case.

6. Or any crimes, court cases or appeals involving the prisoner.
7. Or the prisoner's future plans.
8. Or any matters not covered by Nos. 1 to 7 . . . etc."

There wasn't much left to say. It was the end of a promising career. Not that it would have taken off anyway, as there is not enough space in a crowded cell for literary persuits.

There is only one way to achieve a cell of one's own. To make a formal statement to the governor that one is a homosexual. I was naturally prepared to make such a statement, until I discovered that one was then segregated from all other prisoners and missed out on the Sunday movies and other group activities. With this logic, it means that in the long term, the only sure way to *avoid* homosexual practices in gaols is to state officially that you desire them.

Voluntary isolation would be an absurd price to pay as it's the other inmates who make it all worthwhile. The first lesson is that murderers and rapists are just like you and me—ordinary everyday people, some of whom may be professional crooks and many others arrant amateurs, blown apart on a particular occasion by an emotional hurricane. People triggered off by a set of circumstances into a once-in-a-lifetime freak-out, such as most domestic crime.

The killers I met were often the ones who had eliminated their wives' lovers. It was enough to put me off adultery. I remember one young man who surprised an aspiring cuckolder and blew off one of his legs with a shotgun. He was then having trouble achieving his due parole and kept flunking the psychiatric.

"What do they ask you?" I enquired as we walked to the yard.

"It's always the same question," he replied, "they ask what are my plans when I leave gaol."

"And..."

"I tell them I'm going to blow his other bloody leg off!"

One of the first changes one notices in the nick is the collapse of communications. Words don't mean what they seem to mean any more. They mean whatever the institutions want them to mean. Your first taste is on the day of arrest. A large notice in the police station proclaims your rights. Until first convicted you are entitled to refuse finger-prints. So when the officers prepare your hand for the ink-dip an appropriate stance of defiance is conjured up—but not for long.

"OK you refuse fingerprints and we'll oppose bail . . . vigorously and on each occasion . . . " Oh well, so who cares about a few fingerprints? Besides, I donated them voluntarily at a police exhibition when I was seven.

Another word which leads astray is "hospital", a large barred dormitory under the 24 hour scrutiny of screws and no Dr Kildare. The Largactyl cocktails are distributed to each prisoner before bedtime and the trick is to store enough of the liquid (first in the mouth, then in a secret container) to produce a big bang in the head on a special occasion. In Her Majesty's prisons, drug abuse is the only sure means of escapism.

As another respite from routine, hospital is popular, though inaccessible. Because once you've survived the medical inspection on the night of admission, you're considered able to survive anything. The test involves standing for hours in a cold corridor at night without clothes while waiting for the doctor to arrive, look you over and tell you to hurry up and put on your clothes before you get pneumonia, ha ha.

For most prisoners the biggest shock of all comes at the moment of sentencing by the judge. It's like being hit on the head with a mallet and days later some are still wandering around stunned. I remember being escorted in a daze through the underground labyrinth of the Old Bailey after an exemplary sentence. Behind me the door clanged and I was standing in a huge tiled cell with a whole bunch of defendants from the various cases of the day, most of whom were eerily cheerful.

"What did you get?", asked one.

"Fifteen months," I said.

"What for?"

"Publishing an obscene magazine."

"Christ Almighty!", he replied, "I just got fifteen months too and *I* tried to murder my wife . . . with a carving knife."

It was a warm welcome to a new club.

I never saw him again and by now he should be back in the land of the living. Good luck to you, mate, wherever you are . . . and to your wife.

"Belt up—I'm the one crying for help."

PC 69

HEATH
goes in with the Porn Squad

"I'm looking for a volunteer."

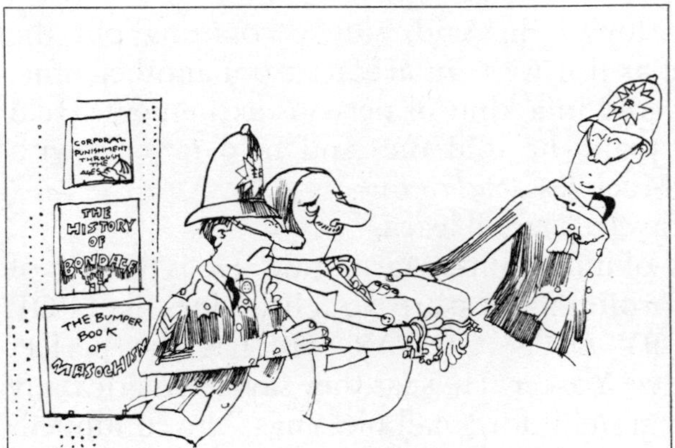

When You and I Were Victims on the Sidewalks of New York

GEORGE AXELROD

THE man at the bank regarded me dubiously. "You mean you want this in *cash?*"

"Please."

"You'll never get away with it," he said.

"Get away with what?"

"With whatever bizarre caper you have in mind. Those idiots in the White House ruined it for everyone. You can't even bribe the *butcher* in cash anymore."

"I live in London now," I explained. "I'm going to be in New York for a couple of weeks. I need some walking-around money."

"Nobody *walks around* in New York! And if they do, they certainly don't carry cash! Even the *Muggers* won't accept *cash*! There's nothing they can *do* with it! Don't you have credit cards?"

"I have a Ladbroke's card. And I think my wife has one for Peter Jones."

"You've been away too long," he said, slowly counting out the money, fingering each note as if it were an artifact from another time. His Zapata moustache quivered in a kind of nervous excitement. He'd been with the bank three years, he told me, and he'd never seen a hundred dollar bill before. Much less *touched* one.

"You'll learn," he said gravely. "You'll learn."

"Take the taxis," a friend of mine called Martin said. He is the sort of man who derives deep and profound pleasure from headlines like: POP STAR ELECTROCUTED BY OWN GUITAR. He has the perfect temperament for a native New Yorker. He's (as they say in America) my kind of folks. "We must be grateful for small blessings," he continued. "A happy rise in crimes of violence against taxi drivers has caused most fleet owners to install a bullet-proof plexi-glass partition between driver and passenger."

"Alas," I said.

"Alas, my ass!" he said. "Not only are these plastic shields bullet-proof, they are also, Praise God, *sound*-proof! Now, one is no longer compelled to listen to the moronic babblings of the driver. Oh, one can still *see* the flapping lips forming words like 'Niggers', 'Mayor Lindsay' and 'Son of a bitch only tipped a dollar!' but because of the screen, the silence is golden—the effect Chaplinesque and almost poetically beautiful!

"Further," he continued (he's a hard man to stop once he warms up to a subject), "the lunatic rise in cab fares has made the use of taxis so prohibitively expensive that one can always *get* one. Even at theatre time. Even in the rain. Of course, once in the cab, you can't *go* anywhere. Because of the traffic. Do you recall the old days, dear boy, when suburban estates were advertised as: *One hour from 42nd Street?* Today, the only place one hour from 42nd Street is 43rd Street!"

"You've been to see *Last Tango In Paris?*" I asked my mother-in-law, a saintly woman of a certain age. "What did you think?"

"Filthy!" she said. She was speaking, I soon discovered, not of the content of the film but of the condition of the flat being offered for rent. "That floor," she said, "had not been hoovered in months! The paint on the walls was peeling! The Venetian blind was a disgrace! What some landlords think they can get away with today! An apartment like that should include carpets and curtains!"

"Was there nothing," I asked, "that struck you as, well, *odd* about the behaviour of the prospective tenants?"

The good lady thought a moment.

"I was married to your father-in-law forty-five years and, except on his gin rummy nights, he always took his trousers off. No, I wouldn't rent an apartment like that if they *gave* it to me. On a ten year lease. *With* the first three months *free!*"

"What's new on the literary scene?" I asked at the bar at *Elaine's,* a revolting and over-priced restaurant in the East 80's where *The New York Review Of Books*-type writers meet to discuss the favourable reviews they will write of each other's books.

"Well, Hal (Harold Robbins, bestselling author of *The Betsey* among other notable works) has just issued an important statement in this month's *Vogue*."

It (Elaine's is a unisex joint and sometimes it's a little hard to determine the gender of the cat you're talking to) handed me the clipping.

"My wife, Grace, chooses all my colognes. In America, she buys Estée Lauder's *Aramis*. In Europe, colognes made by the French couturiers . . .

Rochas, Saint Laurent, Hermes. I have at least two dozen and may use a different one each morning depending on my mood."

"Mary Ann and Steve have invented the most *divine* new party game! It's called SKIN! You take a bed sheet and cut a hole in it, about two inches in diameter. One team gets *under* the sheet while the other team goes out of the room. When the team that's IT comes back into the room, all they can see is this two-inch piece of *skin*! They have to guess not only *who* it but *what* it is!"

"Last week, Norman brought a barbecued chicken from Zabar's Everyone guessed it was Marion's You-Know-What. She just got back from Barbados so it was a *natural* mistake!"

"I hear it's actually *dangerous* to go to the theatre. Or at least down into the theatre district," I said.

"Of course it isn't," Martin said. "But now, at least, we all have a decent excuse not to *go*!"

The hostess was close to tears. I could sense hysteria lurking behind her contact lenses. "Dinner parties used to be so *simple*! Oh, one made an *effort* not to seat ex-wives next to ex-husbands. And it was not all that easy to get a *presentable,* unattached Black Panther at a moment's

notice—they were so much in demand in those days. But now the whole thing has become *impossible*! No one gives a damn any more about who was married to whom; political party, race, colour or creed! Where have all the values gone? The little social graces that meant so much! The art of conversation—gone! All of it *gone*!

"The only thing one's guests are concerned about is DIET! Seat a Dr Atkins Diet Revolution gentleman next to a Harpers-Fourteen-Day lady and the evening is ruined. Carbohydrates! Unemulsified fats! Others insist upon a half grapefruit served between each course! In my day I was taught that if something as ghastly as salmon mousse were served you mucked it around with your fork and pressed on to other matters. Now the simplest dish, *filet de boef* for example, produces cries of 'Murderer!' from the Vegetarians. The fish course is ignored entirely, 'I'd rather eat my mercury straight, thank you.' Jesus, darling, even soya bean souffléd has become controversial! Only the other evening a Congressman from California struck a glass of Margaux '52 from my husband's hand. 'What's the matter with *domestic* wine!' he cried. 'America, Drink It Or Leave It.'

"By the way, darling, you've been away so long I've quite forgotten. Do you take mineral oil or kerosine with your salad?"

"I handle the whole thing in my own fashion," Martin said. (He's getting to be the hero of this piece.) "When the subject of diet arises, as it inevitably does, I silence the table with the following: 'You ever see a fat Vietnamese? Of course not! that's why I adhere strictly the "The Rice and Napalm Diet". Burns unwanted pounds off in *seconds*!' That usually shuts the bastards up at least until dessert. Which I never touch, myself, because of the calories."

The uniformed policeman was standing casually by the smashed window of the Fifth Avenue shop. It was a shop that sold small glass animals.

"What happened?" I asked.

"I guess some citizen wished some small glass animals," he said.

Around the corner, an elderly lady held a handkerchief to her only slightly dented forehead. A uniformed policemen stood nearby, sympathetically writing out parking tickets. "What happened to her?" I asked.

"I guess some citizens wished her purse."

"At least we've run the hookers off the streets," the zealous young man from the District Attourney's Office said.

"Then why don't they just go into one of the Singles Bars?" I asked.

"Probably because they're all married."

Martin, Chico The Horse Player and I were getting outside of a couple of thousand-calorie bacon cheeseburgers at P. J. Clarkes. (To "get outside of a hamburger" is, by the way a marvellous phrase invented by a genius named Dan Jenkins. Credit where credit due. And he wouldn't take cash anyway.) Chico said, "I think this whole diet thing is part of a Nixon Conspiracy. Takes their mind off inflation."

"Sure," Martin said. "A bunch of protein-starved Republicans. They wake up in the middle of the night and they're hungry, right? Starving, maybe. So they got a couple of hundred thousand in cash in a briefcase. But, like the man said, who's gonna take *cash*? Anyway, nothing's open so they gotta bust *into* someplace. Listen, Pally, those cats who busted into Watergate, they weren't looking to bug the place, they weren't looking for the non-existent secret papers, they were looking for the *refrigerator*! A strictly from hunger operation."

The seven-year-old looking man with the ginger-coloured moustache that wasn't quite making it who was standing guard at the immigration-desk at Heathrow at seven in the morning looked at my passport dubiously.

"How long do you intend to stay?"

"*Stay?* I *live* here!"

"Why would an American want to live *here?*"

There seemed to be no possible answer to that. But it was nice to be home.

"We only simmer first offenders."

"Mamma! Mamma!"

"Who are you? What you want with my Joey?"

"Mrs. Frenelli, Joey killed a cop tonight. C'mon, kid!"

"No! My Joey's a good boy. Don't take him. He's a good boy."

"Mrs. Frenelli, we need good boys like Joey in the Mafia!"

HOME GUARD

FENTON BRESLER appears for the defence of private property

SUBTLETY is all. You cannot deliberately kill an intruder, except as an absolutely last resort in desperate circumstances. But if you *accidentally* kill him in the course of using "necessary force"—that's an entirely different matter. Modern law-books still quote the classic words of Baron Parke in an 1841 judgment: "If a man finds another breaking into his house, he has a right to push him out and to use as much force as is necessary for that purpose."

Unfortunately, that does not mean you can frankly own up: "Yes, I meant to kill the blighter." Or: "I couldn't care less what harm I did to him"—which, I must admit, would be my own reaction. Honesty is not advisable in these circumstances. You've got to say: "I only did it to frighten him." Or: "I did not think the boiling oil would really burn him."

With this caveat to satisfy legal scruples, you can, on the spur of the moment, use whichever weapon happens to come to hand. Set man-traps or organised methods of defence come into a different category—and I'll have to come to them later.

Provided you're acting impulsively, you can grab whatever is handy. When, for example, some years ago a Leeds bailiff, attempting to seize goods from a local widow's house, stuck his foot in her front door and tried to push it open, the Divisional Court subsequently ruled she was within her rights in hitting him over the head with a milk bottle. Lord Parker, then Lord Chief Justice, actually repeated the epic line, "Every man's house is his castle."

I cannot refer to any modern case involving the use of a blunderbuss, spiked ball and chain, cross-bow or javelin. But there have been at least two fairly recent cases where the courts have approved the use of swords in defence of one's homestead.

In February 1972, a 31-year-old London householder was awakened in the night by the sound of breaking glass. He took an old military sword from behind his bed and thrust it (like Hamlet into the arras) through the broken window—accidentally killing the would-be intruder standing outside. He told the police he had no intention of hurting the man and thrust the sword through to frighten him away. But their delicate souls did not like the thought of such swashbuckling violence, and the householder was charged with murder.

Mr Justice Cusack, quite rightly, did not even let the case go to the jury. He directed them to acquit at the end of the prosecution's evidence. "If a man is being attacked," he said, "he is entitled to defend himself and his house against the attacker and use reasonable force to prevent the commission of crime by somebody else. This deceased man was an attacker and no offence at all has been committed by the defendant."

Swords were back in favour again at the Old Bailey two years later, when in December 1974 an animal-loving schoolmaster who wielded a 17th-century sword at a drunken intruder, after the man barged into his home and kicked one of his dogs, stood in the dock of the nation's major criminal court. He grabbed the sword and pointed it at the intruder, who ran on to it, he told the jury. Mr Justice Nield directed them it was not illegal for a householder to use a sword "reasonably" to eject a trespasser, and sensibly they acquitted the schoolmaster of any criminal offence.

Your own fists, provided you are young and fit enough, are, of course, a perfectly acceptable weapon to employ. They are certainly easy to handle, after all. In October 1970, the 21-year-old son of a London family woke up to find a 22-year-old burglar creeping stealthily through his room. He jumped out of bed. The two young men fought. It was a vicious fight spilling out into the hallway and ending up on the floor. The intruder died—asphyxiated through inhaling his own vomit. "Death by misadventure" was the inquest verdict—despite cries of "Murderer!" from the dead man's family.

"Had the man not broken into the premises, this would never have happened," said the coroner, Dr. John Burton. "What happened afterwards was the direct consequence of that."

If you can get the gun, you can even legally shoot in defence of your home. Just over fifty years ago there was a classic case in South London: the tenant of a furnished room had been given an invalid notice to quit by his landlady.

He refused to go. So the landlady and her two friends, armed with a hammer, a spanner, a poker and a chisel, beat at his barricaded door. They succeeded in crashing in a panel of the door—whereupon the furnished tenant fired through the hole, and the landlady's two friends fell to the floor with gunshot wounds.

He was convicted of unlawfully and maliciously wounding them. But the Court of Criminal Appeal quashed the conviction. Said Lord Hewart, then Lord Chief Justice, in words which still today remain the law of the land: "No sufficient notice had been given to the appellant to quit his room, and therefore he was in the position of a man who was defending his house.

"In defence of a man's house, the owner or his family may kill a trespasser who would forcibly dispossess him of it, in the same manner as he might by law kill in self-defence a man who attacks him personally; with this distinction, however, that in defending his home he need not retreat, as in other cases of self-defence, for that would be giving up his house to his adversary."

His late Lordship was only being highly logical. In defending yourself from personal attack, you have in theory to be a coward. You should not at once strike back. You can only retort with violence after first showing your lack of willingness to fight. The position was put with commendable clarity in a 1969 judgment of Lord Widgery, the present Lord Chief Justice: "It is not the law that a person threatened must take to his heels and run, but what is necessary is that he should demonstrate by his actions that he does not want to fight. He must demonstrate that he is prepared to temporise and disengage and perhaps to make some physical withdrawal."

It sounds like a perfect description of Harold Wilson's political credo. But, in any event, it does not apply to defending your home. You haven't first got to give it up before you try and get it back. You can strike or shoot first—then ask later. But, of course, nowadays it is very difficult to get a firearm or shotgun certificate out of your local police authority. It seems to be official policy to let only professional criminals or political terrorists obtain firearms with ease.

Whatever the traditional view of the law may be, the police themselves do not seem to like the idea of the ordinary citizen emulating John Wayne. I have always felt considerable sympathy for Spike Milligan about that remarkably stupid case of his some eighteen months ago when, appalled and fed up by continual police refusal to do anything effective about curbing damage done to his garden by local young hooligans, he took a non-lethal ·177 pellet air gun and fired at a 16-year-old youth who was trying to scamper off his property.

Needless to say, nothing seems to have happened to the trespassing intruder but poor Mr Milligan was hauled before the local magistrates and only let off with a conditional discharge after a homily from the Chairman of the Bench about society "not condoning the use of loaded weapons against other people". I would have thought myself that society should also not condone desecration with total immunity of private property.

But then the law has long drawn a distinction between what Professor R. F. V. Heuston has called "retributive" and "deterrent" methods of house protection. You can legally "deter" intruders by such accepted means as barbed-wire fences, spikes and broken glass on top of walls and iron bars on your windows. But you cannot resort to "punishing" burglars and trespassers by anything which seems to savour of retribution for their wrong-doing.

It is all terribly English—and pussy-footing. You can arguably set up a complicated system of electric wiring on your outer fence—but only if you display large and easily readable notices all over the place warning everyone that is what you have done. When the new Guard Dogs Act came into effect, sharp-toothed guard dogs remained legal—but only if you displayed prominent warning notices.

The rules of cricket pervade the scene. As long as the chap knows what he is letting himself in for, the law does not mind too much what set methods of defence against the intruder you avail yourself of. The one thing you must not do is take the poor benighted chap by surprise.

Nor is this generosity of spirit a modern phenomenon sired by the blessed principles of the National Council for Civil Liberties. It is the Offences Against the Person Act of 1861 which says: "Whoever shall set or place any spring-gun, man-trap or other engine calculated to destroy human life or grievous bodily harm, with the intent that the same or whereby the same may destroy or inflict grievous bodily harm upon a trespasser or other person coming in contact therewith" commits a crime punishable by up to five years' imprisonment.

The Victorian legislators made one exception to this anachronistically milksop rule. "Nothing in this section shall be deemed to make it unlawful to set or place, or cause to be set or placed, *from sunset to sunrise,* any spring-gun, man-trap or other engine in a dwelling-house for the protection thereof," they said. But just you try and get a firearms certificate out of the local police! I don't much rate your chances, even quoting this ancient Act. Pea-shooters and cap pistols are more in line with modern official thinking.

A SIGN OF OUR CRIMES

A Crime and Motion Study of New York City's idea of fun, almost based on exhaustive research notes — but they were stolen from ARNOLD ROTH

Burglary and Stealth

Orthodox Crime Prevention

Unabashedness

Corruption in High Places

The Common Rip-off and The Protective Ploy

Social Awareness

Home Insurance

SNUG AS A BUG

MILES KINGTON

THE exhibition at the United States Trade Center last week might well have been called "The Human Villainy and Wickedness Show". What it was actually called was the "US Industrial and Commercial Security Equipment Exhibition", which in English means the latest American gadgets for stopping human villainy and wickedness. My mission: find out by any means possible the lowdown on the gadgetry. My problem: gaining access to the closely guarded Trade Center.

At 10·29 a.m. I casually approached the front door.

"Can I help you, sir?" said a well-built man moving silently out of the shadows.

"I have come to visit the exhibition," I said.

He nodded and moved back into the shadows. Inside the front door a man in bright blue security uniform held up his finger.

"That package," he said.

"It contains no guns, tape recorders or electronics," I told him. "Only unfinished TV sketches and a novel title."

"I'd leave it in the cloakroom if I were you," he said. "Don't want to hump it all round the show, do you?"

Halfway to the cloakroom I was stopped by a young lady who asked me to fill in a form. Before I realised what they were up to, I had given them my name, line of business, executive position and revealed who had sent me. She typed swiftly and stuck on my lapel a large placard reading: "Miles Kington, Assistant Editor, *Punch*". It wasn't going to look good in my report, admitting they'd got all the facts out of me before I'd even started.

Inside, things were tricky. Rows and rows of stalls, displaying "Multi-Access-Point Data Security Systems", and "Controlled Wave Pattern Transducers" and "Solid State Photo-Electric Battery-Powered Smoke Detectors", and nothing in English anywhere. My eye fell on a familiar object. It was a TV set. On the screen there was a familiar face. It was me. I moved on hastily and went up to a stall at random.

"What is it?" I said, pointing at a shiny length of chain.

"It's a bicycle padlock," he said. "We built it so strong, that it's too heavy for bicyclists. So we toughened it up for use as a motor bicycle padlock, and then found that many motor bicyclists, attracted by the long chain and heavy ball at the end, were hitting each other with it. So we've withdrawn it from the market?"

"Great. What next?"

"This." This was another, longer chain, with lock. "You can attach it to any typewriter, piece of office equipment, desk-top computer and chain it to the floor. Protects against sneak thieves, drug addicts and organised crime. We guarantee the cash value if it's stolen."

"So it's not fool-proof?"

"Nothing is fool-proof. If you try hard enough, you can break *any* security system. If man can make it, man can break it. All that anyone here is doing is buying time, making things more difficult for the villain. You can never make it impossible. You ask them."

At the next stall there was a notice saying "Ultrasonic transducers no longer need have an ugly appearance. The low profile and ruggedized construction make these heads the most vandal-resistant in the industry". I noted it down. I'd always wanted to know how you spelt 'ruggedized'. A siren went off in my ear. Some damn fool was demonstrating an emergency exit alarm. I went to the stall beyond.

"Are you buying time against criminals?" I asked.

"No, I'm representing Maxalloy."

"?"

"Very, very hard metal. Guards the vulnerable parts of safes."

"But if man can make it, man can break it," I quoted. "True," he said respectfully. "You have to respect the professional criminal. He'll spend months at a time figuring out just one system. He'll go to university courses in electronics. By the time he has mastered one device, it's time for us to think of something new. Look at this."

This was a tungsten carbide saw-blade.

"It's marketed openly in America and can cut through anything, because they've found a process of attaching carbide chips to a metal blade. So we had to produce this."

This was a huge lock which took two hands to lift.

"You cut through that and halfway you come to six strands of our own carbide chips. They're bigger than those on the blade, so we strip theirs off."

"What about bugging—is that your field too?"

"Sure. We undertake debugging. It's easy enough, just establishing the presence of electronic devices, but it takes time to trace them. A boardrroom can take two hours to debug, or three days."

"Can a board of directors be sure of security if they meet in the middle of a field?"

"Not really. Telescopic mikes aren't that hot, but you only have to toss something near the speakers and you've got a pick-up immediately. Failing that, there are always lip readers."

"!"

"Sure."

People do strange things in their spare time. For instance, they change figures on cheques before paying them in. That's why ProtectoGraph have perfected a method of printing, embossing and staining cheques. They go into factories after hours when they shouldn't. That's why people make machines that detect body radiation, that detect broken sound waves and that take photographs at 100 yards, *in the dark*. (Developed from an American Army night-time rifle sight.) They rob vending machines. That's why the Illinois Lock Co. has produced a lock which you can change instantly. They also try to gain access to high control areas. But Indentimation, from Northvale, New Jersey, have licked that one.

"Based on computerised analysis of glove measurement for Air Force pilots," recited my contact, "we have worked out that hand measurements, dimensions and pressure vary from person to person, like finger prints. We can code a card for an authorised person, based on his hand, and to gain access to the area of security he had to put the card *and* his hand into the Identimat-2000. One is useless without the other. So if someone steals the card, he can't use it, because he hasn't got the right hand to go with it. It's foolproof."

Foolproof? But if man can make it . . .

"No way. It's foolproof."

But what if you, well, to put it bluntly, wanted access so badly that you cut off a man's hand and used it?

"Quite apart from the extremely illegality of it, we don't think that a dead hand would work. We haven't tested it. Volunteers were not forthcoming."

You could perhaps bribe a card-owner and his hand?

"Ah, that's the thing to remember. The best weapon to beat security with is a corrupt employee. But who has the money and resources to improve human nature?"

As I left the Trade Center, a siren went off. The exit alarm again. My bicycle was still there outside. But I had taken certain security precautions, notably buying such an old muddy bike such that unauthorised persons would see only a low profit threshold in the operation of knocking it off.

Back at HQ, I was about to file my report when an idea occurred to me. I went to see the General Manager.

"As a matter of interest, have you ever had our board-room debugged?"

"No, we haven't. But a few months ago we lost ten chairs from it. All in one night. We have since taken certain security precautions."

"Oh?"

"Yes, we now have board lunches standing up."

I think he was holding out on me.

"The thieves don't appear to have taken anything."

CLUNK, CLICK, EVERY TRIP!

JOHN STONEHOUSE's prison journal

THE idea, fostered by the television series *Porridge,* that prisons are natural joke factories is badly wide of the mark. Television fiction, we all know, is often a distorting mirror on Society. To be fair, Mike Yarwood gets perilously near the truth in his chosen field of political impersonations but he, wisely I would guess, steers clear of prison themes.

The humour inside those forbidding walls, which only the chosen minority are allowed to enter, is of a special ironic kind. It takes the newly initiated some time to appreciate it but, when he does, the realisation helps him to cope with his own dreadful plight. To be deprived of one's liberty is a terrible shock. My first experience was in Australia last year. After fruitlessly petitioning the Queen to be allowed to return to Westminster to attend the House of Commons where my fellow members were about to expel me for non-attendance, I told the Melbourne Court that, willy nilly, I simply had to go. Predictably, at Melbourne airport I was arrested for attempting to leave the jurisdiction of the Victoria State courts and despatched to the notorious Pentridge gaol.

And so I had my first bitter taste of prison. It was a shattering experience and hardly alleviated, at the time, by the thought that one is following in the footsteps of Nehru, Kenyatta, Makarios, de Valera and others. Only one's fellow inmates provide the sounding board for seeing the funny side of things. That is why, I suppose, solitary confinement is considered the worst possible punishment.

My turning point came because of a macabre joke. I shared a cell with five Australians. They took delight in putting me in a corner bed, where an unfortunate prisoner six months before me had died in tragic circumstances. His head had been completely severed in an axe attack by his cell mates. Believe it or not, after that I slept extremely well at night in the knowledge that, whatever my predicament, I was better off than some other poor soul. Needless to say I had checked out that I did not share my predecessor's cell mates.

I then had the privilege of being sent to Her Majesty's Prison at Brixton, after the Director of Public Prosecutions, on instructions from the Attorney General, had portentously opposed the granting of the bail which had been allowed me in Australia. As with all horrible events in one's life—once they are over—it was an experience not to be missed.

Brixton is a century-old cluster of monstrous structures originally built for women and then redesigned for a few hundred male prisoners. It is grossly overcrowded. On Friday, thirteenth of February, Dr Shirley Summerskill, that delightfully inoffensive lady who has special responsibilities for prisons at the Home Office, confessed that all local prisons are overcrowded. Brixton is worse than most. The so-called official Certified Normal Accommodation, to be henceforth known in this age of confusing initials as CNA, is 649. Brixton at the last count had a prison population of 1,049. It is thus 400 men and a grotesque 63 per cent overfull.

Grotesque conjures up the image of a hideous monstrosity. The word can also mean odious, loathsome, foul, barbaric, uncouth and absurd. How else to describe an institution where men, simply because they are denied bail, are kept locked in small cells—mostly three to a single cell—for 22½ hours out of every 24? When their trials are finally held nearly half of these men will either be acquitted or given non-custodial sentences. They would have sacrificed their freedom for months and, in some cases, for over a year. In that time most would have lost their jobs, and some their wives, in the dislocation that imprisonment inevitably brings.

Living cooped up with two other men in a tiny cell for months on end is not supposed to be a punishment, according to Dr Summerskill. Let me assure her that if it is not punishment, most of the men suffering from it would prefer the real thing. For life inside Brixton is incredibly barren. Apart from the regulation half an hour of exercise in the mornings and afternoons and a "B' movie show on a Sunday every fortnight, there is no recreation. The word "exercise" by the way, is a misnomer for it consists merely of shuffling around a yard disgustingly fouled by the Alsatian guard dogs.

The only other times prisoners are allowed out of their cells is for the occasional 15-minute social visit, a solicitor's interview, to collect food or to slop out. The latter is a ritual which must be unique to British gaols, as most foreign prisons have given inmates access to water-closets. Even Pentridge, also a century old, has concealed W.C.s in every cell.

At Brixton men are never allowed out for calls of nature. One evening at about eight and some days after my arrival there, I rang the bell in my cell to call the gaoler on duty. Foolishly I thought, as my need was urgent, I could use one of the two W.C.s nearby. I was in for a rude shock. "Nonsense," said the gaoler, when he eventually came to speak through the Judas spy-hole. "You can't get out until seven in the morning. I don't even have a key to the cells when I'm on night duty."

"What can I do then?" I asked.

"You can use the chamber pot, that's what it's there for," he said.

In the cells where there are three or four men together, they share a bucket. At slop-out times there is a mad rush to clean out the various receptacles and as there are only two toilet basins on a floor for upwards of 100 men, the congestion is appalling. It does not make the situation more pleasant that the only place to wash eating utensils is in the self-same restricted area.

The washing arrangements are awful. Only five showers for nearly 300 men in "C" wing, and the ration is one shower a week per man. It is arranged that the men take their allocated shower on the afternoon before the weekly court appearance a remandee has to make before his committal trial. The Magistrates' Courts would smell pretty badly if they did not take this precaution, especially in the long hot summers when Brixton becomes quite fetid.

The food is dished out to prisoners at 7.15 am, 12 noon and 4 pm, but as there are no dining areas it is eaten in locked cells by men crouched on their own bunk beds. The cost is £2·60 per week per prisoner. Much fun is made in comparison of the fact that each guard dog has £3·45 spent on his weekly food. Remandees can have food sent in and that helps to improve variety, but as all the packets are emptied on to plastic plates in the vain routine search for files, much of this imported food rapidly becomes unappetising. As a concession to civilisation half-a-bottle of wine can be sent in daily but this delight is somewhat spoiled when the receiving officer pours it into an ill-washed jug which only lately held milk or Ribena.

The gaolers are called "screws" by the inmates. Generally an apprehensively affectionate relationship subsists between them, although both sides could produce candidates for the most brutal mercenary gangs in Angola. The abiding impression of the prisoners is that Brixton is certainly not run in their interests. On every available opportunity they are locked securely away so the screws can have their cups of tea in peace and quiet. From 4 pm (Dr Summerskill will say 5 pm) the cells are "banged up" until 7 the next morning. For most of that 14-hour stretch only one gaoler is on duty, without keys, to watch nearly 300 men in one wing. It is difficult to imagine that the proportion of prisoners to staff is three to two in British gaols, when it is necessary to keep the inmates locked in tiny cells for so long.

Critics of British railways, or any other nationalised service, say the staff regard the customers as a damned nuisance who only get in the way of running the enterprise. In Brixton at least the staff can put their customers out of sight, and largely out of mind, for 94 per cent of the time. It is a triumph for syndicalism.

"Understand, we avoid any premises where the burglar alarm isn't ringing."

Knees-Up in the Nick

From which DAVID MYERS steals quietly away . . .

"All day I've been pounding the ruddy beat . . ."

"I thought you'd like to know that the bloke whose hair you ruffled while you snipped off his tie and stuck olives in his ears was the chief constable."

"That's Sergeant Potter who's saved countless young girls from the sordid clutches of Soho."

"I'm just not having the neighbours see you in that disgusting condition."

. . . to see how the other half celebrates.

"I hear when he's wearing his stocking he's quite good looking."

"George was going to get me the matching ear-rings but he was disturbed."

*"Perhaps that will teach you **not** to invite people like us."*

"Actually tonight's do doubles as a farewell party for Big Louie."

"I'm ready to go home, Bert— whip out and nick a car."

Softly, Softly, Catchee Copper

As members of the police find themselves on the wrong side of the charge sheet, JONATHAN SALE makes a statement

WHEN a pair of trousers and an envelope containing five clerical outfitters' catalogues fell out of my saddlebag on the way to work, it wasn't a Cambridge criminologist or a Civil Liberties official or a petty thief out on bail, or any others whose views I normally take into consideration, who picked them up. It was a police constable on the beat whom I have to thank, and a couple of his colleagues who set off, possibly under the impression that there was a vicar without his trousers in the vicinity, to tell my wife that all was not lost.

The debt that we owe to coppers is enormous, and I speak for us all, not only for those of us who want to change our trousers when we have cycled to work and write articles on clerical fashions. But it is a debt that we don't pay by maintaining a complete silence on the unacceptable face of the boys in blue. There is great annoyance in police circles when the Press pitches into coppers caught with their wallets open, or when Sir Robert Mark hots up his campaign into corruption in the force; but there is a limit to how much the positive side can be played up and readers might tire of too many stories beginning, "Late last night our Crime Reporters discovered shattering evidence disclosing that 99·99 per cent of London's top coppers are not implicated in Soho's porn racket!"

Individual cases aside, there is no doubt about police porn rakeoffs, according to those in the know, such as observers like an acquaintance who is straight out of Damon Runyon but built in this country under licence. "In all my years in clubs in the West End," he said, "I never came across a single straight copper." But he turned out to be the police's staunchest supporter—not that they would thank him for it—on the grounds that while they would turn a blind eye to what doesn't do any harm (forgetting Lord Longford for the moment, if not longer), violence would be jumped upon immediately. Payments started, but on a purely voluntary basis: "It became a regular feature, like the rent. It started as a tenner a week in 1960, and now it's £50—that's inflation for you—going to about 200 people. I would say there is a minimum of 15 grand a week involved."

According to my back-of-the-lorry pocket calculator, this means that 75 separate businesses are concerned in these financial transactions, and the whole operation is worthy of Stock Market quotation, since three-quarters of a million pounds a year are involved. These figures can't be checked, in the absence of any company report on the lines of: "Detective Constable Jones in his Chairman's statement told shareholders that profits before, not to say without, tax totalled £2,500 in the last twelve months of trading. The loss of business following the closure of Dirty Mags 'N' Pix in Frith Street was more than compensated for by the opening of its subsidiary round the corner, Reg's Films Ltd." But there is no question about the existence of rakeoffs, and, indeed, of coppers whose salary is augmented by illegal freelance work.

Don't take my word for it, don't take the word of an Underworld, un-named contact. Listen to the evidence of Sir Robert Mark, who recently boasted that since he became headmaster, 82 members of staff have been expelled, while those who jumped before being pushed average 75 a year; in the previous decade, both categories totalled a mere 16 a year.

"Dammit, Christine, you know I'm as blind as a bat in forty denier."

Take the evidence of convictions in court, which have the advantage of being incontrovertible and quotable without fear of libel. Take Ronald Hales, a detective chief inspector who offered to forget about some drugs in return for £10,000 and was shopped by an indignant pusher who denounced him with some justification and more irony as a "gangster". Take Robson and Harris, picked up by sleuths not from Interpol but *The Times*, for extorting money that sometimes totalled sums of the magnitude of £25.

Take the grand catalogue presented by the Underground legal magazine *Up Against the Law* in its recent special issue on "One Bad Apple". This is a round-up of theft, assault, blackmail, shoplifting, transvestism, wife-beating, careless driving and being drunk and disorderly on a pilgrims' flight to Lourdes, all compiled from court reports and all concerning policemen, labelled for handy reference by name, rank, offence, and, indeed, rank offence.

And it is this that shows the prevalence of corruption among policemen, not just for the volume of cases but for the low level of reward for which they are prepared to risk their careers. The rich pickings of Soho and drugs could cause a normally honest man to stray, but anyone who is caught with his fingers in the till for a few quid can have few standards at the best of times. He would be the sort of policeman who goes round to arrest a thief and helps himself to anything valuable while he's at it. This actually happened to a criminal I knew; his wife told the officer that the watch which had walked off was not, oddly enough, bent and that there was a receipt to prove it; the detective didn't know what she was talking about, but later the watch materialised in her letterbox.

That isn't admissible evidence in the case against the police—now it can't be told, we don't name the guilty men—but it remains true nonetheless. And I could take Robert Mark to a man who was laying a carpet in the auditorium of a large building one night, when a fairly senior member of the uniformed branch strode in and demanded that he trot round to the officer's house, carpet it throughout, and report the missing pieces stolen. When the poor craftsman refused on the grounds that the carpet couldn't be removed without implicating him, the guardian of law and order retorted, "All right, your van is obstructing the traffic"—of which there is a great deal in suburban sidestreets during the early hours—"and there's a car park two miles away. We'll be following you to make sure you drive there, but you are quite free to walk back in your own time." Of course, the carpet man would have forgotten all about it when Robert Mark and I knocked on his door, but again it shows that if a policeman will put the arm on an innocent stranger for a few yards of material, there can be no holding him when the stakes are high.

It is the CID, moving without the protective colouring of uniform through the twilight world of informers and wealthy villains, who are most at risk. Mark has been nibbling at the autonomy of this branch, to the dissatisfaction of its members, and he has been accused of lowering morale by ferreting around where the odour of corruption lingers. To this he could reply that it was hardly his fault that such ferreting is necessary. If making investigations and taking action lowers morale, then the Richardsons and Krays could complain that their morale had been seriously tampered with. Mark knows there are bent policemen around, the public is beginning to know there are bent policemen around, and bent policemen know there are bent policemen around. Stating this is not an attack on the forces of law and order.

It will doubtless be said that this article hasn't made the work of the police any easier. But then the police don't make their job any easier. It is better to make a fuss now than allow a slide that leaves us with only the option of turning to criminals when the boys in blue are robbing us blind. What worries me is a state of affairs in which the police don't return my trousers and clerical catalogues but take them down to the flea market, or, worse, prise them from my saddlebag themselves.

"Never mind the simple tricks he's taught you. Has he mentioned the airport bullion job yet?"

To The Rattle of an Underwood

STANLEY REYNOLDS

IRELAND, land of song and poet, has always found it difficult to produce bad writers. But Ireland did produce the New York City police force. All they can write are traffic tickets.

In London right now—London which saw the verbal explosives of Wilde, Yates, Shaw, Synge, Joyce, O'Casey, and Behan—we have been witnessing a most curious new form of the Irish prose style. I refer, of course, to the regular confessions of Irish rebels which are spread in joyless and pallid prose across our Sunday newspapers. Miss Maria McGuire, late of the IRA, was the first to sell her secrets to the London papers. Her confession appeared in the *Observer;* and not one word or phrase of it caught my eye or struck my inner ear. Now it is the turn of a Mr. Big Dave Fogel, who fled Ireland and the UDA and ran straight for London, Fleet Street, and most of the front page and all of pages 16 and 17 of the *Sunday Times.* Judging from this generous example of Big Dave's prose style, I think he could get a job writing tickets for speeding in New York any day of the week.

Another interesting angle of these Sunday paper breast-barings is that Miss McGuire and Big Dave are, actually, when you come right down to it, nothing but informers, which, of course, is in the great Irish tradition as all of us who saw John Ford's *The Informer* on BBC2 the other night know.

But what a different life the informer has in the 'seventies compared to what poor Victor McLaglen went through on Channel 2 the other Sunday. There he was as Gypo Nolan, skulking about in the Dublin fog, afraid to show his face to so much as a stray dog. No TV press conference for Gypo. Begorra, informin' was man's work in them days.

I don't know what a couple of full pages in the *Observer* or the *Sunday Times* are worth. But I'll bet they'd knock spots off the 20 quid poor Gypo got for singing to the Tans back in 1920. An' sure now, reader darlin', ever since I read Big Dave comin' clean I've bin havin' th' most pehrplexin' dhreams with John Millinton Synge all mixed up with Sean O'Casey and all goin' off like thunder-claps in me oul' brain.

The scene is a cottage kitchen. A turf fire on the right. A couple of tinkers, stage left. A pig with black feet. A couple of weather-beaten blind beggars and their wives. A fiddler. Old and young barefoot persons in shawls. Half a dozen assorted men in belted mackintoshes who intermittently clean their Thompson guns and sing colourful and incomprehensive ballads. At curtain's rise PEGEEN, the daughter of the house, is seated down centre at a table slowly composing a shopping list. Her Da, Commandant Costello of the IRA, sits by her side.

PEGEEN (*slowly, as she writes*). Six nice bombs for to blast th' Tans. A nice pair o' pistols. (*Looking up.*) Tell me, now, Da, are we all out o' gelignite entirely?

THE DA. An' sure now, Pegeen, didn't th' pig with th' black feet be afther 'atin' it, along with them sticks o' th' T.N.T. an'm me own self's bes' boots.

PEGEEN (*as she writes*). A nice economy king size bag o' th' jelly it is t'en, an' a hondhred round o' th' dum dum bullets. Th' kind what yiz dotes on, Daddy daarlin'. But sure now, Da, there mus' be betther ways o' making' a livin' then goin' out in th' penethratin' cold an' thrampin' up an' down lookin' for Tans to take pot shots at. Gettin' yiz poor oul' self all pehrished with th' col' an' penethrated with mud. Daddy daarlin'.

Enter MAURYA, the mother, or rather, the mither, of PEGEEN. Six sons she has brought into the world and five of them have been lost to her and she is none too sure of the sixth, BARTLEY, who has been showing a dangerous penchant of late to ignore his Thompson gun and bombs while spending most of his time mooning over an old Underwood typewriter composing letters to Fleet Street Press Lords.

MAURYA. Pegeen, where's yiz brother? Aren't I afther tellin' th' fella to mind th' pig with th' black feet before it 'ats anny more TNT (*noticing Pegeen writing*). Be God, girleen, what's that yiz whritin'? It's not! O, God Almighty, no!

PEGEEN. Hush now, mither, it's onny th' oul' Satiddy shoppin' list. A few rounds o' th' ammo for th' Da, a bomb or two, an' a couple o' bags o' th' jelly. A daarlin' blast it'll make, wooshin' an' bangin' an' fillin' th' air with dazzlin' catherine wheels o' flyin' morthar an' concrete.

MAURYA. T'ank th' Dear Lord an' Saint Aloyisus o' Parma an' Saints Dolores an' Maria Concepta an' th' Blessed Mary Margaret Clitherow for dat, daughter. Begorra, I was afther t'inkin' yous was writin' to th' *News o' th' Worl'* like that poor misbeguided brother Michael o' yourn. Michael! Me son, me son, me poor boy, where are yous now?

PEGEEN. Yiz know where he is, mither—writin' the' filum script o' his confessions for Misther Robert Bolt, starrin' Misther Robert Mitchum, mither daarlin'.

THE DA. Hush yous mouth, Pegeen. I tol' yiz never to mention that scud's name under this roof agen. Betther he was dead than to do what he done. I raised a pack o' spies, pimps an' informers cantherin' at me heels, an' I'm afther gettin' a terrible twinge in me right leg! I'll have to have a dhrop of intoxicatin' liquor though I hate it, I've no pereeogative.

MAURYA. Oh, me boys, me sons! Michael off to th' *News o' th' Worl'*, Sheamus writin' for th' *Observer*, Patch tellin' all in th' *Sunday People*, Stephen appearin' wid Mary Holland on th' London Weekend TV, an' poor darlin' Shawn, daarlin' Shawn, th' apple o' his mither's eye. I doted on him. He was me dote. Lost forever to the *Sunday Mirror*, leavin' me here cryin' an' lamentin'.

PEGEEN. Hush now, mither, hush. Yiz know what Docthor Rooney was afther tellin' yous th' night o' th' bad attack wan he came, th' good docthor, th' daarlin' man, gallopin' to yiz rescue over the meadow where th' purple wild flowers grow an' th' golden jonquils are heavy in th' evenin' with th' twinklin' weight o' th' dew an' hang their heads over like shy counthry girls at a dance before th' fiddler strikes his bow. Remember what th' docthor said when he come ridin' to yiz wit' th' sparks flyin' off o' th' hoofs o' his good bay mare, th' one that was in foale last Spring an' won th' two mile at th' Sligo Fair a summer ago but one where I wore me straw yellow bonnet wit' th' pink ribbons an' I danced all night wit' Philly O'Cullen to the music of t'ree fiddlers fiddlin' wild an' wicked like a maddening dog lying in a ditch. Keep takin' th' tablets, the docthor says. An' rest aysey.

THE DA. Yerra, it's a fine blessin' on a man, sunk in age with' his head hangin' heavy wit' th' cares an' th' cross words o' th' world ringin' in his two ears, to be havin' a fine daughther like yous, Pegeen, daarlin', wit' a fine command o' th' cursed English language slippin' aysey an' light an' lovely from yous tongue full o' flavour as a nut or a shiny red apple on a leafy green tree in the middle o' June. O, me twinge! O, me twinge. A dhrop, daughter, darlin', a dhrop daarlin'. (*Angrily*) Not like dem rapscallions o' brothers of yous writin' them joyless an' pallid paragraphs in th' London press. Simple declarative sentences creepin' across o' th' pages like a pack o' limpin' convalescents. A dhrop. A dhrop. O, me twinge. Th' pain in me leg's blowin' a terrible tatheraraa.

PEGEEN (*soothingly*). Hush now, Da. Take dis hand grenade left over from what th' pig with th' black feet didn't eat an' go out an' blow up th' post office. It'll do yous good an' ayse yiz sorras. An' here's t'ree bob for a pint at Mooney's on yiz way back, Da.

(*Exit the Da pursued by the pig with the black feet.*)

(*Enter a barefoot lad waving a copy of the* Sunday Express.)

THE BAREFOOT LAD. It's Bartley, Missus Costello. He's all over the *Sunday Express. (The boy reads from the newspaper)* "I have left the I.R.A. I found it was not for me. Who would have thought that I, Bartley Costello, son of Commandant Costello, who was raised with a Thompson gun at my mother's knee, would want out. Today I reveal all about my life as one of the 'boys'. I will tell all. Just the way it happened, simply and with no frills. See pages 15, 16, 17 and 18."

MAURYA *(falling to her knees).* O, Bartley! O, Michael, Sheamus, Patch, Stephen, and Shawn! All me sons! What was th' pain I suffered, Bartley, bring yous into th' world compared to readin' this? Sean O'Casey, John Millinton Synge, Brendan Behan and Misther W. B. Yates, sir, have pity on us all. Take away them simple declarative sentences an' give us th' glory o' parenthetical phrases an' poetical digressions. Take away this murdherin' English syntax, an' give us Thin own eternal mixed metaphors!

(A loud explosion is heard off stage. Enter a second barefoot boy.)

SECOND BAREFOOT LAD. Missus Costello, Missus Costello, th' pig with the black feet has just exploded blowin' up th' post office, Mooney's, the Commandant Costello an' all in a great an' ear-splittin' conbustalation of trotters, hide, curly tail, grunts an' squeaks and soarin' flesh an' mortar—

MAURYA. Come, Pegeen, darlin', get out th' typewriter, there's nothin' left now but to get it all down for th' Sunday papers. *(Dictating to Pegeen.)* It's strange to think that I, who nursed my sons on the glories of the Irish language, would ever be writing dull stuff like this, but . . .

CURTAIN FALLS SLOWLY

Is There a Spy in Your Street?

MAHOOD has a few words of sympathy for those brave men faced with the thankless task of trying to extract secrets from the British

"Dammit man, surely by now you British should have developed a camera capable of giving a sharp picture of a power station in a thick fog."

"I don't like it Comrade Ivanov—nine out of ten of them positively ***want*** *us to sabotage Concorde."*

"One can't even stop to take a photograph without some nosey parker wanting to know if they can help—why can't the British mind their own business?"

"First things first, mate—before we discuss the espionage, we have to settle the rate for the job, annual guaranteed increases, pension rights, arbitration procedure, redundancy payments, differentials, demarcation . . ."

Typical British efficiency—their damn Xerox isn't working."

"Our blackmail plot fell foul of their permissive society, Natasha—you've been swapped for Mrs. Braithwaite."

What Are Your Twelve-O?

As the Criminal Justice Bill to reform the jury system chugs through Parliament and the arguments around it blow up once more, ALAN COREN takes the typewriter in his right hand and swears to tell as much of the truth as the law allows

IN the century-and-a-half since Henry Brougham sharpened his quill and came to the conclusion that "he was betrayed by his fancy into no metaphor who once said that all we see about us, Kings, Lords, and Commons, the whole machinery of the State, all the apparatus of the system, and its varied workings, end in simply bringing twelve good men into a box", a considerable number of this country's citizens have shuffled into stout oaken pews and sent their peers to chokey. And, of course, during the same period rather more of them have seen fit to find the defendant not guilty and bung him back on the pavement either to continue to lead a blameless life or to retrieve his jemmy from the cistern and recommence operations behind a broad smile.

No-one who has filed into court to pass judgment, as I have been doing for the last few days, can fail to have Brougham's stirring tropes engraved on his consciousness; or, at least, their gist. Because the bizarre truth about justice in England (and a sizeable whack of the civilised world, too) is that, for all the robes and gowns and wigs, for all the decorous courtliness of language with which the professionals thus dolled up address one another, for all the nuances of precedent and gobbet culled from the towers of law books that stand upon the polished benches of our learned friends, for all the quaint oaths and snatches of dead language and procedural flim-flam, the filter into which all this expert and eon-hallowed stuff is painstakingly poured is actually a small mob of labourers, housewives, clerks, and, occasionally, humorists, who up until that time have never heard a Latin tag spoken in anger, nor realised that Rex v. Grimsdyke was anything other than a match between two little-known members of the Third Division. To see a couple of articulate QC's volley at one another for two days, only to have the whole thing settled inside half an hour by a dozen blokes with that morning's *Sun* sticking out of their dungaree pockets is a weird experience; as if, say, one were to commission Cecil Beaton and David

Bailey to photograph a coronation, and then send the film to Boots for processing.

There must have been two hundred of us assembled on that Tuesday morning at the Inner London Quarter Sessions; nominally representative of this queendom's proles, of course, but *de facto* (amazing how one picks the stuff up) nothing of the kind. For a start, under the present system of selection, we were all householders of one sort and another, a qualification which instantly excises from consideration some eighty per cent of the women of England. Of our two hundred, perhaps ten were skirted. Furthermore, privilege, position, rank, influence and, indirectly, money still being the thriving things they are, the citizens mobbing the lobby that morning were largely those who were unable to dodge the column: managers, proprietors, executives and all others capable of drafting a note explaining their indispensability at their place of work having previously (unless their social conscience had pricked them to atypical depths) dropped a line to the relevant Sheriff and been excused. Add to this the fact that doctors and lawyers are automatically exempt, and you will not be astonished when I tell you that a fair number of those present would have had to work in teams to come up with a complete alphabet. Nor, I sincerely hope, will you start running off at the tempers about my snobbery, or whatever you choose to miscall it; you're regular readers, most of you, and you know me better than that. Humanity is not measured in IQ. Intelligence is, though.

Anyway. All being assembled, a Jury Bailiff barked a few terse syllables at us, a couple of his gowned sidekicks poked us into a more or less orderly line, and we were marched off into Court Number One with all the dignity of sheep going into the dip. Considering that we were the cornerstones of the English legal edifice, official courtesy was somewhat patchy; and to shouts of PUT THAT CIGARETTE OUT! and STOP GIGGLING! and NO TALKING THERE! the rocks upon which is built a juridical meisterwerk that is, so I understand, the envy of the world, were piled in the aisles. And left for half an hour; during which time the crowd around me weighed up the pros and cons of those engaged in the 7.45 at Walthamstow and drew moustaches all over Rupert Murdoch's nudes, shrieking until silenced by the surveilling beaks. It grew hotter and, surreptitiously, smokier. Discipline wavered. Men started sidling off to use the lavatory without first asking permission, and official wrath began to wax.

At last, just as the whole tableau was beginning to take on the lineaments of a Hogarth doodle, a skeletal man appeared, wig askew, and gave an impassioned speechlet on the sanctity of the jury system.

The last cliché having rung round the Edwardian beamery, the moralist slid back into the panelling, and an NCO took up the story.

"Right!" he roared, "When I say your name, come down here!"

The names boomed out, warped by the dread acoustics; and, as the ethnic structure of our regiment became apparent, so too did the irritation of the shouter. There were, for example, about half a dozen Irishmen with the same name (which I am not at liberty to divulge), and time and again the proceedings were held up while three or four blokes made a dash for the door or got wedged on the stairs with their namesakes; furthermore, many of the prospective jurymen having been summoned from Shepherds Bush, there were large numbers of names like Mtasi and Ngartha which the caller was incapable of pronouncing and the echoes incapable of conveying, with the result that everyone kept asking everyone else whose name had just been called out and consequently not hearing it when it was called out again.

I never got to hear mine called. When ten juries had been empanelled and thundered off down the various dark corridors, the rest of us were counted off and told to wait in the restaurant, a hall with a tea-urn at one end in which some forty or fifty men happily trooped and formed into fours for solo. It was now eleven a.m.; we had been summoned at nine. At twelve-thirty, a lunch menu was pinned up, with its heady alternatives of boiled beef, bangers, or cod and chips. It was something to do.

"May I have some lunch?" I said.

"Did They say you could?" she said.

"No," I said.

"Then you can't," she said.

At one o'clock, a gown came in and released us for lunch. As one, the men got up and began to troop out. I asked one what they knew that I didn't.

"Topless go-go down the World's End, innit?" he said.

It had an edge over remaining alone with the dead cod. I followed.

The pub lies about two hundred yards from the Court. When I arrived, it was packed from skirting to cornice with jurymen, barristers, policemen and, no doubt, numerous bailees and villains, locked in sweaty camaraderie that transcended all those fine hair-lines of the legal compass and watching a short nude whose bust probably went back to the great days of F. E. Smith and Marshall Hall. At five to two she ladled everything back into her bra, and the custodians of British justice turned on their heel and trudged out into Newington Causeway, and back to Court, just in time for the afternoon session.

If you were working, that is. No trials having finished, and no vacancies in consequence having come up, I was replaced in the canteen, and enjoined not to move on pain of all sorts of things to do with Her Majesty's Displeasure. At four p.m., They threw me out.

"Well?" said my wife, whom I had left that morning with the impression that what she was seeing stride down the hall was the right hand of God. "Was it a murder? A gangland vendetta? A fraud that may bring down the entire Cabinet?"

"I am afraid I am not at liberty to discuss it," I said.

"Can't you say anything at all?" she said.

"Gin," I said.

I was back the next morning. The lobby was buzzing with illegality as those who were engaged upon cases left hanging from the previous day gloated over those who'd slept in the canteen, in the sort of detail against which they'd been specifically warned. I sought the Bailiff, and enquired as to my duties with a politeness that has been known to melt granite.

"You wait till you're called," he said.

Amazingly, I was. Withing an hour, and the GLC cheese roll still stuck in my oesophagus, I and seventeen other souls were led towards a Court, twelve to be permed from eighteen. The Bailiff glared at a man beside me.

"Where's your tie?" he hissed.

"At 'ome."

"It's not a bloody holiday," said the Bailiff. "You come properly dressed tomorrow."

We filed into Court, which was already brimming with periwigs and coppers. Two very short defendants stood in the dock. The judge came in, sat, and we sank with him.

"I shall call the names of the jury," shouted the Clerk, "and any objections must be made before they take the oath."

He peeled the names off, and the citizens took their place. At the seventh name, the only woman juror, the defence counsel challenged.

"Why?" said the woman.

Stunned, the Court stared at her.

"You may not ask why, madame," said the Judge.

The woman, who had obviously had her hair done for the occasion and who took the challenge as personal criticism, glared at him and stood her ground. After about three enormous seconds, the Bailiff touched her on the arm, and she bristled out.

Twelve jurors were called.

I was the thirteenth.

"Go upstairs," said the Bailiff.

I went upstairs. The cardplayers in the canteen glanced up briefly, noted that I was not a call to work, and glanced down again.

"This is the life, eh?" said one.

"Yes," I said.

"They're going to pay us for all this tea, you know," he said.

At three-thirty, the Bailiff woke me up. I peeled my face from the Formica beside the codbones.

"You can go home," he said.

"ALAN COREN!" he cried, on the third day.

We trooped off. I brightened, felt duty beckon: it might be arson in Her Majesty's shipyards, a forger of Tintorettos, an expatriate Sicilian dope-ring. I had been called to represent and protect society as we know it. I would weigh, ponder, mete.

"It's you again," said the woman with the hair. It was metallic pink this morning.

"Yes," I said.

"I'm running out of dresses," she said. "And it's ever so hot for suits, isn't it?"

"I hope it's rape," said a giant in a mildewed cap. The Bailiff pointed at this item.

"Take that off," he said.

The gentleman in the dock, who had waited, we learned, for eighteen months for his case to be heard and who now stood surrounded with an army of judicial talent, was accused of dishonestly taking away copper pipe to the value of £1·50. The copper pipe lay on a table in a brown paper bag. It and its various owners, permanent and temporary, were discussed for two days, the latest beneficiary having claimed, as a building labourer, that someone had said it was all right for him to take it off the site. Eight hundred years of legal history were brought to bear. Miniscule points were adduced, policemen long since transferred were brought from Leeds and Portsmouth. There was no evidence worthy of the name. At last we retired.

I am not at liberty to divulge what took place in the jury room. Other than that one of our number stood convinced of guilt, on account of the man had funny eyes, she said, and a face like a weasel. At the other extreme, another good man and true refused even to consider the evidence, maintaining that, as a labourer himself, nicking copper scrap was not a crime and never had been, everyone did it, didn't they?

For two hours we thus argued from fixed principles, totally ignoring

"He owns Shanty Town!"

everything that had been ground out over the previous days. Whenever I fought to get them back to the concrete stuff in hand, they glowered at me; and whenever we seemed to have arrived at a verdict, eleven of us half-rose, only to have the question of the weaselly face brought up by the sitting member.

Eventually, we wound our way back, found the defendant Not Guilty. The policemen shot us a dark look or two, the defendent sniffed, his counsel smirked, all rose, His Honour shuffled out, and we, it being still afternoon, were despatched once more to the canteen.

Where everyone immediately agreed that the bloke was actually guilty.

And where, two days later, I still am. No doubt I shall be called soon, to pass judgment on some fearful nosepicking case, or an attempted smoking on the lower deck, or a case of an unlicensed dog that strikes at the very roots of all we hold most sacred.

Meanwhile, I have plenty of time to think. And one of the things I most think about is this: if justice must not only be done, but also be seen to be done, how on earth do you reconcile this with a system in which twelve unqualified laymen are allowed to come to daft private conclusions in utter secrecy, are not allowed to give their reasons for so doing, and are not held responsible for actions based not upon evidence but upon ignorance, prejudice, carelessness, and having to get home in time to put the dinner on?

I don't know what effect these men will have upon the enemy, but, by God, they frighten me.

Oh, not to be in England, now the bombs are there!

SEAN MAHOOD and the rest of the non-combatant Irish in England try to keep a low profile during the troubles

"My God, Seamus, you don't think they're trying to ***price*** *us out of the country?"*

"I don't object to being searched going ***in*** *to the office building but now they're searching me coming* ***out****!"*

"A loan, Mr. McNulty? Have the American and Colonel Ghadaffi let you down?"

"If you ask me, Paddy, they brought their damn dog to sniff for gelignite!"

'This is Patrick Kelly speaking on behalf of Kate, young Mike, Spot the dog and myself. We wish to disclaim responsibility for the outrage just announced!"

"Sean would like to fraternize but he just doesn't **know** *any Irish jokes!"*

"You have a very Irish face, Mr. Ryan, just like all the Photofits."

"They're sick and tired of their every phone call causing a bomb scare."

The Gilded Cage

Being the penal reforms of JOHN WELLS

A NEW method of cracking down on violent crime that could shake the Underworld to its foundations has been proposed this week by ninety-seven-year-old Judge Knott, the drug-addicted Cointreau-sodden doyen of High Court society whose witty summings-up in rape and murder trials have made his name a household word all over Latin America. Judge Knott, an amateur psychopath and keen dribbler, has come out with the controversial suggestion that all those convicted of violent acts should, instead of going to prison, be recruited into Military Hard Labour Battalions where they would have a bit of sense knocked into them with weighted pick handles and be trained to serve the public as Judges and Policemen.

According to the Judge's proposals, the convicted criminals would be taken from the court, forced to have their heads cropped by rude Mayfair barbers and obliged to exchange their comfortable prison uniforms for starched collars, tightly-braced pin-stripe trousers specially designed to cut them under the chin, movement-restricting black waistcoats and jackets and target-style bowler hats, ensuring that any convict trying to escape could be picked out and stunned by low-yield nuclear missiles. They would then be drilled in small squads to march in a dignified manner over measured stretches of pavement in the City of London, put through gruelling courses in alcohol consumption, blowing through empty briar pipes and exhausting small-talk, and ordered to consume a set number of heavy dinners under the supervision of specially engaged bores. They would then be confined singly in leather arm-chairs with copies of *The Times* of the day before, and taught to make a series of simple ejaculations, whistles and clucking noises.

After five years of this the convicts, deprived at all times of ordinary human society and treated with injections of special ageing and doddering hormones, would be equipped with uncomfortable horse-hair wigs, red nightshirts with obtrusive white fur accessories, and be set to work in high wooden cages, filling in forms, asking questions, and reading out hysterical denunciations of society interlarded with blood-curdling curses and condemnations.

One convict who has already served for several years in a "guinea-pig" capacity, dressed in a furry guinea-pig costume, wig, ermine and plague posy, confesses that his nerve is beginning to crack. "Stone-breaking, knitting mail bags, being forced to drink ten gallons of water and then being jumped up and down on by Mrs Margaret Thatcher, all that is nothing compared to the humiliation and boredom I have suffered. Thrown among men whose minds have been warped by drink and their many years on 'the Bench', many of them of overtly heterosexual leanings, it was inevitable that I should feel myself becoming more and more sullied and degraded. But being exposed in public in 'the Wig'—no, that is too much. If I ever get out of this red flannel strait-jacket it is goodbye to crime, I am telling you."

Equally harsh is the treatment reserved for those drafted into the police. After being photographed for identification in "publicity" pictures showing them in police uniform in the company of an effeminate-looking person brushing clues off a steering wheel with a tiny paint-brush, they would be exposed to "idealists", sometimes in groups of up to five hundred or a thousand, who they would be required to "assist with their enquiries". They would then be subjected to intensive psychological readjustment, during which time certain suggestions about their nature would be made to them by objective observers, and relodged in separate mud-filled billets where they would be required to roll on their backs, grunt, and repeat the words "Oink Oink". Those who survived would be put through a rigorous course of arm exercises and called upon to pit their wits and skill against simulated hooligans and homicidal maniacs in fast cars who attempted to "run them down". At no time would they be allowed to come into contact with criminals, and those who weaken would be dragged through unsavoury "hippy penthouse flats" by growling alsatians. Few can stand the strain, and applications for transfer from those who have already been sentenced, either to the more "lucrative" upper reaches of the Force or to Devil's Island, have been numerous.

As Judge Knott himself says, spinning about in his jackboots and screaming into the battery of dummy microphones in his bathroom, "The Backlash is coming. I don't know who it's going to hit, but by God they're going to take a thrashing."

Spaghetti Alla Mafia

William Davis

HE looked like a worn-out Anthony Quinn—dark-skinned, unshaven, pot-bellied, sad. His eyes were bloodshot, and the hand that raised the half-filled glass of wine was shaky. His jacket was stained with the remnants of countless forgettable meals. His name was Rosario Terrasi, and he was the chief of his local Mafia. Or so the judge in Palermo had said.

"They took me from my 18 grandchildren," Rosario wailed. "I never even had a chance to say goodbye."

We were on the tiny island of Filicudi, a respectable distance from the east coast of Sicily. Few people had ever heard of the place until Terrasi and fourteen other alleged Mafia chiefs arrived there some weeks ago. They were arrested in a dramatic swoop, and dispatched to Filicudi under an Italian law which permits the banishment of "undesirables" even if they have still to be tried and found guilty. The one hundred and ninety-seven islanders promptly abandoned Filicudi in protest, and returned only when Rome promised to send the Mafiosi men elsewhere. They are now in Sardinia; I was there when the islanders waved them goodbye.

On this hot afternoon, a few days before they left, Terrasi was sitting outside the Hotel Sirena. The Sirena has seen better days, but that isn't saying much. As we talked, the other Mafiosi joined us one by one. They were bored, and we offered a break in a dreary routine.

To understand the Sicilian Mafia (whose influence is almost entirely confined to the western part of the island) one has to accept several basic facts: the long history of corruption, the widespread distrust of officialdom, the poverty of much of the population, the superstitions of ignorant peasants, the Sicilian's devoted pursuit of power through fear, and the deep-rooted belief that real strength lies in loyalty to family and friends. Sicilian pride is often absurd, and violence lies close to the surface, but the Mafia continues to exist because it is based on a way of life. Mario Puzo's best-seller, *The Godfather,* is set in America, and the America of several decades ago at that. But Don Corleone is impressively real. "Does this man have real balls?" he asks his *Consigliori* before tackling a rival, and Puzo explains what he means: does he have the courage to risk everything, to take a chance on losing all on a matter of principle, on a matter of honour; for revenge? The *Consigliori* is made to put it another way: "You're asking if he is a Sicilian."

I did not find it difficult to visualise the fifteen Mafia men of Filicudi as the entire cast of *The Godfather*. Even Terrasi, despite his unimpressive appearance, fitted in. He was less smooth than his city colleagues, but one could see him oozing sentimentality one minute and being utterly callous the next. If someone got hurt, he would smile sweetly and explain that it was entirely the victim's fault: he shouldn't have got in the way. The others looked even more convincing. There was Calogero Sinatra (yes!), a sly, intelligent-looking man who looked capable of anything. And Giacomo Coppola, a thick-set, aggressive type proudly displaying an immensely hair chest. And Antonio Buccelato—a short, powerfully built Sicilian who shouted every word and underlined his arguments with swift karate chops that made the heavy table tremble. And a quiet, white-haired man who wouldn't give his name, but told me in excellent English that he despised the communists but adored the late Winston Churchill "because he knew what he wanted, and got it." And a slim George Raft type who, despite the heat, was immaculately dressed. And an old man with a limp who appeared harmless until my companion, a photographer from Milan, suggested that he was lucky to be in Filicudi because the sun was shining and the sea was wonderfully blue. The old man suddenly turned violent and lashed out with his walking stick. For fully ten minutes he heaped abuse on the world, and the Italian Government in particular. He had been arrested by mistake, he hated the place, they wouldn't let him see a doctor, there was no justice, and all journalists were swine. He would make everyone pay for it as soon as he got home.

It was all very convincing. But, of course, appearances can be deceptive. I always thought that Humphrey Bogart and Jack Palance made utterly convincing villains—more so than, say, Al Capone. And the head of the police force guarding the Mafiosi confessed, with a grin, that when a foreign television crew had found it difficult to get enough Mafia men together for an interview, he had stepped into the breach. Who, after all, would know the difference?

Coppola and Buccelato invited us inside the hotel for a beer, and for the next two hours we had a heated discussion. There wasn't a policeman in sight, except for the obliging commandant, dressed in sweat shirt and an old pair of trousers. "We can't," he explained, "have policemen walking up and down in the sun." Buccelato nodded agreement. "We and the police," he said, "understand each other." He went on to claim that he'd been arrested because he was making a lot of money, and people were jealous. He was a nice chap really, a family man whose brother was a Monsignore. How could anyone possibly think that he was a Mafioso? "There is no Mafia in Sicily," he declared. "They only use it as an excuse." He was "like a little stone thrown into a well." He couldn't claim to be an angel, but if he and the others were really Mafiosi they wouldn't be in Filicudi. "The real Mafia is sitting behind beautiful desks, with servants opening their doors for them," he said. "If you want to find the true Mafia bosses, look at the closest friends of politicians."

Coppola (accused of being involved in an American drug ring) also claimed that they were being offered up as a sacrifice. "If they make a show of arresting people like us from time to time," he said, "they can leave the real villains alone." He was bitter about the islanders who, he said, had been "very insulting." They were treating them like monsters. "Children run away from us," he said. "I tried to offer one some money and his mother pulled him away. One small boy even asked me if it was true that we eat children. My God, we have children of our own!"

Buccelato said it was high time that the Government formed a body which could establish what a Mafioso is. Was a man who took bribes, in return for awarding someone a profitable contract, a Mafioso or just a clever businessman? Was a fellow who got into a fight, in order to defend the family honour, a Mafioso or merely a decent, upright Sicilian? Was a corrupt politician who used his office to advance his own interests a Mafioso, or simply a man who recognised that if you don't look after yourself in this harsh world, no one else would do it for you? "If Jesus had been born in Palermo," he added, "he would have been a Mafioso too." He hit the table to emphasise his point, and ordered another round of beer. We could see that they were really quite decent fellows, couldn't we? Did we think they were capable of killing people? They loved their little children, and missed their homes. They had been unfairly treated, because Italy wasn't a civilised country. It couldn't happen anywhere else in the world.

We finished our beer (the eager hotel proprietor insisted that it was "On the house") and said goodbye. Eight of the Mafiosi insisted on accompanying us to our boat. "Come again tomorrow night," they said. "We'll get some fish and cook dinner." The commandant nodded agreement, and they all waved until our boat was out of sight.

Around the corner, on the other side of the island, some of the local tradesmen confessed that they would miss the Mafiosi. There had been a lot of talk about Filicudi losing tourist trade, but the truth was that there had never been much of it anyway. They had put up a sign "Tourism is our bread" for the benefit of television crews. The Mafiosi had done for Filicudi what Ingrid Bergman had done for Stromboli. Millions of people around the world had heard of Filicudi for the first time. They would come to see where the Mafia chiefs had stayed. And they would eat spaghetti alla Mafia—a new dish just invented by the best cook in Filicudi (garlic, parsley, oil and red pepper). Who knows, one might even be able to sell some Mafia souvenirs.

The Mafia chiefs, they went on, were not really such bad fellows. Some of the islanders actually regarded them as heroes—though, of course, it didn't pay to say so. Look how many policemen it had taken to bring them to Filicudi!

We tasted the spaghetti alla Mafia, and decided that the tradesmen were right. The protests had been unnecessary; Filicudi had collected a fortune's worth of publicity. We also decided that, if Mafia meant corruption, the world was full of Mafiosi. The Mafia was, in Barzini's phrase, a "many-headed dragon" and bigger heads than Terrasi's and Buccelato's were going free. Not least, we reflected that the most effective weapon against secret organisations like the Mafia is ridicule. The Mafia's power depends on fear. Make them look big, and you enhance their prestige. Laugh at them, and people will laugh with you.

"Thanks to inflation we'll have to mug 20 per cent more people this year just to break even!"

ARTIST IN CLINK

LARRY looks behind the sudden boom in prison paintings

SELECTION COMMITTEE

TURPS

Eight Hours in the Nick

BASIL BOOTHROYD and HEATH assist the police with their enquiries

SATURDAY afternoon, King's Road, Chelsea. Wet, crowded, getting dark. "It's better now they're down in the second division," says the constable at the wheel, braking politely to let a fellow motorist pull out from the kerb. We aren't going anywhere in particular. Not yet. Not until the skull-cracking stream of intercom messages throws up something for Bravo One. Routine patrol in an area car, blue light off, no siren. The driver is sparing with the siren's bray. "I live in these parts, I know what it's like."

Our driving is exemplary. If we're stuck in traffic, we're stuck like anyone else. Besides, even a mild infringement of the highway code could trigger complaints from alert members of the public. Bad police behaviour. Full report and investigation inexorably to follow.

"Let's hope they stay in the second division." The inspector, in the front passenger seat, laughs to show he doesn't mean it. Diplomatic. I could be a Chelsea fan.

He's a great laugher, anyway. Compact, wiry, going a bit grey at thirty-six, he's just been in paroxysms, with tears starting, over recollections of violent encounters. He's alive to the pleasing irony: as when a mob closed in for a kicking, he hunched himself to take it, nothing else to do, and a couple of old cons with broken bottles waded in and got him out.

"You didn't recognise me," he said to one of them. "No?" said the man. "You got me four years." The second rescuer, just to round things off, happened to have been sent down by the inspector's brother.

I'd been advancing a private theory about the policeman's lot: that he's doubly cut off from the common run of humanity, first by the closeness of his social circle, consisting preponderantly of other coppers, second, because all his working contacts are villains. The first is more or less true. But, on the second, all baddies aren't wholly bad. And even when they are, as any SOCO, or Scene of Crime Officer, will tell you, the kindness shown their victims by friends, neighbours, even

Racing through King's Road traffic!

strangers, is beautiful and surprising.

He was at Brixton then, for that near-booting. (Boots are the commonest offensive weapon. Steel toecaps. There are knives, axes, brass knuckles and so in the miniature museum in Chelsea station . . . also a mock-gelignite bomb, with alarm-clock convincingly attached, found on a scientifically-minded 13-year-old . . . but they're falling from favour.) Here at Chelsea, there's marginally less blood. Nothing sensational going on today, for instance, just a murder investigation and a double suicide. But what there is tends to go on all the time. The area is commercial *and* residential. Lots of money around. When the shops shut, from Harrods down, and the stream of shoplifters is stemmed, the clubs get going, the well-lubricated private parties. There'll be nothing like a hush before 5 a.m., and a few lingering drunks still to be scooped in.

Shop-lifting is hell. Rife isn't the word for it round here. The only consolation is that not all stores have store detectives. If all thieves were spotted the thing couldn't be handled. It sounds nothing, but it's a prime time-waster. The store dick telephones the bad news, a car has to be diverted. In goes the officer. Is there a case? It's up to him. If so (and it's usually so), and he makes the arrest, he'll have to see the whole business through: back to the station, detailed statements, charge sheet in triplicate, distressed weeping if this is one of those lady offenders with a purseful of money who can't believe she did it. He can be out of useful circulation for hours—and in the witness-box tomorrow, which is just too bad if he's due for a day off or a late shift.

My first car was diverted for a shoplifting. I felt a sense of heavy, undefined responsibility, waiting outside the store for the constables to reappear. Sober in charge of a police car. They brought out a very nice suede jacket ("Wouldn't mind one of those myself," said the driver), and a very tall coloured gentleman of noble bearing, bearded, in an ankle-length leather coat and fur collar which must have cost a packet. Well, might have cost a packet. The other constable escorted him into the van which had discreetly arrived behind us. When we made it back to the station to pick up a fresh oppo for the driver, the alleged wrongdoer was in the charge room, waiting in a small queue, chin up, composed, princely in dignity.

That's how I got the inspector in the passenger seat, next time out. He shouldn't have been there, but there was no one else to go.

The first question you want to ask inside the police station is where the police are. There should be 150 or so. From the Chief Superintendent, who is also the boss of "B" Division besides running Chelsea, through half a dozen inspectors to the rank and file. All I saw beyond the counter of the station office was the Station Officer, a sergeant, intently telephoning; and a constable writing in an enormous book. Back a bit, a couple more, on ceaseless give and take with radio messages. In the CID room, ten or twelve well-papered desks, all vacant. One detective constable, in a sports coat, just gathering some of the paper and leaving at speed.

Part of the answer is that there are three shifts, "reliefs", in station language. So on this one, 1400 to 2200 hours, we have one-third of the establishment. Less, because of rest days, sickness. And less than that, because the strength is well short of the establishment. The rest of the answer has a sudden obviousness. This year, so far, they've brought 3200 charges at Chelsea. Call it ten a day. You don't find your lawbreakers inside the station, anyway until you've brought them there. So where the police are is out working. Earning themselves busted rest days in court, very likely. That's one of the annoyances of the job, never being able to make a private engagement with any certainty of being there. Wives find it trying. The divorce rate is high.

And arrests and charges are only a bit of it. Rare consummations. There's often nothing to show, in return for time, energy, not to say courage. Bomb scares. The car intercoms are choked with bomb scares. I suppose we got a dozen. Not all for us. Other cars would take. "Bag on railings." "Beer barrel on pavement." "Suitcase in doorway." You have to go, and fast. This could be it. Then, decision. Clear the area, cordon off, call the bomb car? This is on permanent stand-by these days: one sergeant, two constables, specially trained in the urban bang. You get there, decide the bag is just a bag, the barrel just a barrel. Or they aren't there any more. Perhaps never were. Or they're piles of rubbish. Or, of course, bombs.

One of our messages said laconically, "Car exploded," and gave the location. I think the driver said, "Oh, God," but the siren was on by then, and his foot well down when the laconic voice came back. "Cancel your one-o-zero-eight, Bravo One. Bogus call." We ease up, switch off the two-tone. "Happens all the time," says the inspector, immensely calm. But he's lit a cigarette, and holds it below window level between discreet puffs. He feels guilty about that. In uniform. Shouldn't be doing it. Wearing uniform all the time is a strain, he says. Partly the physical feel of it. Chiefly because it takes every eye. Impeccable behaviour at all times. No relaxing.

On the other hand, it exerts a strange power over the public. Young policemen take time to learn that. Called, say, to a pub fight, their impulse is to rush in and separate the two contenders. "So what happens? They get thumped by both." The experienced man walks into the bar and watches from a distance. He's soon spotted. The Law's here. Nine times out of ten, the fight just fizzles.

Young coppers learn from old coppers. Not from sergeants, inspectors, certainly not from training courses. The sooner they learn, the better. The pity of the system is that it's always the young ones, perhaps of only three or six months' service, who are eyeball-to-eyeball with your actual villains. With promotion, the policeman progressively retreats into supervisory and administrative functions. Experience gets locked up inside the station, shuffling lots and lots of paper. There seems no solution, but it's a shame. It's during the first year or so, still vulnerable, that the young ones tend to drop out, pack the job in. It takes time to grow a shell, resistant not only to physical attack, but to witness-box grillings by counsel for the defence. That can dishearten deeply, accusations of frame-ups, planted evidence, falsified statements from the accused. When you've done your damnedest, and by the book, and have to take an hour or two of this kind of thing, you want to hang up your helmet and get out. Lots, unfortunately, do.

Still, it isn't all violence and villainy. (Or even calumny by lawyers—who sometimes apologise afterwards for giving the lad a hard time, and if he sticks it long enough he'll realise it's all part of the game, sad to say.) There's a good deal of cosseting and comforting. "We do more welfare work than the welfare workers," someone said over a quick coffee in the section house, without resentment. Some old dear rings up the station in a state, says she's frightened but can't say why. Perhaps there's been a break-in lately somewhere nearby. "PAAOTC", scribbles the man taking the message. "Please allow an officer to call." He does. She makes tea. For ten reassuring minutes there's this policeman, symbol of security, and she simmers down. "All right now, love?" So it doesn't only happen on *Z-Cars*.

The real policeman is largely tolerant of the TV fuzz programmes. What makes him laugh, though, says my inspector, laughing, is that the villains always get done, and there's a wealth of manpower. Always raise a dozen at the drop of a helmet. Those are the great splits between fact and fiction.

Or there are burglar alarms always going off in the shops and offices, probably for no good reason, but you daren't risk it. Some just clamour locally, and passers-by report. Some are linked direct to the Yard, and whipped into the Chelsea radio and out to the cars from there. CSASOP, says the message form. "Central station alarm suspect on premises." Result, usually SOIEBLO. "Set off in error by lawful occupier." There's animal trouble. "Dog in shop bitten several people." Result: "Dog returned to owner, nobody bitten." Enquiries flood in. Is

this Chelsea resident, in trouble elsewhere, good for bail? A 16-year-old girl from Chicago is known to be around London, SW3, please attempt to trace.

But the word most repeated is "disturbance". It squawks out all the time from the five R/T channels in Bravo One, and can mean anything. You won't know until you get there. One of our disturbances was a mugging, old gent knocked over for £190. He thought there were three men. No description. We drove around in the dark. Nothing. What can you do? Other disturbances were domestic. Reported screams. Just a family disagreement. One came through as a "serious disturbance", and we put the light and the siren on for that. It was stimulating to go screaming through the red lights: even more so, when our lane was blocked, to scream through them on the right-hand side of the road.

The driver finds the address in one. He and the inspector are out like bullets. "Whatever happens, stay in the car," they tell me. They needn't worry. As an afterthought he shoves the microphone at me. If they're in trouble I'm to press the button and say—laconically, of course—"Police urgently require assistance, 158 Uverdale Road." Too bad. They come back at the stroll. Only seems to have been a husband-wife punch-up after all. I'm disappointed. so is the supporting car that screeches up just as we're leaving. Our driver waves an apology. "Cancel. No trouble." "You owe me a cup of tea on that," says the other driver. "I've just steamed through two miles of solid traffic."

As for us, we steam back to base. A diversion or two. Nothing much for us. Notting Hill tube (disturbance by football supporters) is off our patch. We could look for trouble. A matter of personal initiative. "That woman in the yellow coat, eyeing the men," says the inspector. "I might decide she's a soliciting prostitute. But then again, I might not." I feel my totally unfounded suspicions rising. We drive on. That bit about promotion being pegged to arrest-statistics, by the way, is all bunk.

Back at the nick again the clock was coming up to ten, and the relief booking on. In the briefing room, a formal display of laid-down equipment, 1 truncheon, 1 whistle, 1 notebook, 1 pencil. Stylised. *Pirates of Penzance*. Personal radios now being signed for. The relief inspector was going through our eight hours' documentation. There'd be overlaps, just as there were when we'd come on.

It hadn't been spectacular. Handbags left in cabs. Shoplifters, shoplifters. Suspect bombs ad infinitum. They'd still be looking for the old gent's muggers. We'd located "person missing from guided tour". Couple of traffic hit-and-runs, one hauled in. No trace "suspicious blue Fiat back of Harrods." Disturbance 38 bus. Man arrested with stolen credit cards, *and* cannabis found in his possession, an undesired complication. Mild soccer aggro today, as Chelsea hadn't lost to Plymouth (hadn't won, either: 2–2).

But something rather nasty from the football ground. Detailed statement of complaint from a citizen alleging wrongful accusation of drunkenness by a Chelsea officer, and forcible removal from the ground after he'd paid 75p to be there. This means a Chief Inspector's investigation. Worse, if use of unlawful force is upheld. That's assault.

The inspector is pleased to be away on time for once. Now hatless, trendy in a lightweight black leather jacket, he gets us by car to Victoria, where we both take off on our separate ways.

No, he says, shaking hands, he hasn't got tomorrow off, Sunday. It's the fourth rest day in succession to go down the drain, he can't remember why. Oh, one was a demo, one was catching up on arrears of paper, there was a suicide, and he'd had to come in for the inquest. I sympathise, and he laughs. "You *pay* me, you know."

He can take his pension at forty-four. Not that I can see him doing it. I rather hope he doesn't, the way things are going.

BLACK MUSEUM AND DUTY PARADE.

As a service to Russian agents everywhere, who might otherwise spend a good deal of time and energy trying to chat up British newspapermen, we print this . . .

Russian Agent's Complete Guide To The British Press

"Soviet agents are very active in the press world, in Fleet Street : . . and bearing in mind the amount of effort they devote to these areas . . . one must suppose they find them profitable." —*Ex-head of MI5, talking to Franks Committee.*

"This year, at least one well-known Fleet Street journalist has been fired because MI5 proved to his editor that he was a paid Soviet agent."
—*Chapman Pincher, Daily Express.*

"The Russians try to discover our (journalists') sources so they can judge whether they can trust the information that is printed." —*Chapman Pincher.*

1. The principles of British journalism are exactly the opposite of those of scholarship. A scholar spends much of his time adding footnotes, bibliographies, brackets and appendices to show exactly where he got his information from. A British journalist spends much of his time *removing* any trace of the sources of his stories. To start a story "The Government expects soon to introduce measures which will radically modify the structure of" seems to him much more praiseworthy than starting "I was buttonholed last night by the Minister of Trade, who asked me to leak details of certain measures being planned by the Government to see what reaction there would be. In return he promised to tell no other lobby correspondent. The measures, for what they are worth, are . . . "

The second story is, of course, much more interesting, but no British journalist in his right mind would use it.

2. I am afraid I cannot reveal how I acquired that information.

3. I can reveal, however, that I did not pick it up in El Vino. El Vino is sometimes said to be the great HQ and gathering place of Fleet Street

writers. This may have been so in the past, but now the place is stuffed full of lawyers. If you fall and break a leg as you enter, the nearest five tables will leap forward offering to sue El Vino for negligence. There are still one or two regular journalists, it is true, notably Philip Hope-Wallace who, as you will know, is the new head of MI5.

4. I am afraid I cannot reveal the source of that information.

5. I can, however, reveal that this guide for Soviet Agents was originally the idea of the editor of *Punch* who, as you will know, is in Soviet pay. The intention is to blacken the name of as many Fleet Street writers as possible by suggesting, for instance, that Philip Hope-Wallace is the new head of MI5. In fact, Mr. Hope-Wallace has not been head of MI5 for many years now.

6. The well-known journalist whom Chapman Pincher reported as fired by his editor because he was a Soviet agent is Hugh Cudlipp, who "retired" last month. My source for this information is a man who used to work for IPC and knew Hugh Cudlipp's secretary quite well. Or said he did. Perhaps he was a Soviet agent.

7. When checking the truth of any story in a British paper, you should look out for the secret sign whereby journalists indicate whether or not the story should be taken seriously. If a story is printed baldly without qualification, such as "More than thirty people were killed in a train crash in South Africa last night", then the story undoubtedly has some basis in fact, even if it turns out to be two serious injuries in a plane crash in Angola. If, on the other hand, the writer is not sure there is any basis for his report, he slips in a key phrase such as "It can reasonably be assumed that", "We can be fairly sure that" or "What seems to have happened is that".

8. There seems no reason to doubt that the well-known journalist fired for being a Soviet agent was Bernard Levin. His pieces, it is true, still appear in *The Times* but they are produced by a computer specially programmed to mount the bewildering parentheses and Wagnerian eulogies that Mr. Levin used to specialise in. He was, it can be reasonably assumed, fired for supporting the American presence in Vietnam, a policy which plays straight into Russia's hands. What seems to have happened is that the editor noticed one day that Mr. Levin was the only man left in Britain who supported the Vietnam offensive.

9. Last year more than 8,000 items of news were exported from Britain via the Russian Embassy. Nearly 6,000 of them concerned the imminent collapse of the British economic system and had been planted there specially for export to the Soviet bloc.

10. I am afraid I cannot reveal my source on that one.

11. As you read this article, it is being photostated in the Russian Embassy and rushed off to Moscow just in case it contains trustworthy information.

12. The well-known journalist fired for being a Soviet agent was Lord Chalfont. He now works on *The Times* where he ghost-writes the articles signed by Lord Chalfont, a well-known politician but badly-known journalist.

13. The NATO plan for countering a Russian air attack is in the third drawer down, Room 307, Ministry of Defence, under the September *Playboy*.

14. Quentin Crewe has recently left the *Evening Standard* spot as restaurant critic. He had consistently advocated frequenting expensive restaurants which, he suggested, provided better food than cheap restaurants. This policy, if followed by all his readers, would speedily have led to the bankruptcy of many of the more discerning members of the British public. He is not, however, the well-known journalist referred to as a Soviet agent by Chapman Pincher.

15. Will the person who borrowed the September *Playboy* from room 307, Ministry of Defence, please return it, together with the funny maps and charts that were underneath, which can be of no use to the finder but are of great sentimental value to the owner?

16. British newspaper security is probably the best in the world, thanks to the system of D Notices. These are documents containing secret information which are passed to newspapers with orders not to print them. From there, they are passed to the Russian Embassy by Bernard Levin, Lord Chalfont, Hugh Cudlipp and others, though not by Quentin Crewe.

17. There was, of course, no well-known journalist sacked this year for

being a Soviet agent. This was a pure fabrication by Chapman Pincher in order to lower morale among Fleet Street writers. Chapman Pincher, the well-known journalist, is, as you know, a Soviet agent.

18. Although many British journalists are recruited to Russian intelligence work after they have reached a high position, some agents are planted as apprentice writers at an early age and work their way up through an organisation. The writer of Jennifer's Diary, for instance, a column in *Harper's Queen* which viciously satirises the stupidity and frivolity of the British upper classes each month, and exposes them to ridicule in a series of revealing photographs.

19. You must not make the mistake of assuming that all seditious talk in British newspapers reveals a Russian agent at work, or that all information is wrong because it is inefficient. It can also be deliberately wrong. British counter-espionage is a highly skilled operation, and it is almost impossible to recognise it when it is at work.

20. THIS IS A BRITISH COUNTER-ESPIONAGE DOCUMENT. PLEASE PRINT IN PUNCH ON OCTOBER 11TH. HOPE YOU ARE KEEPING WELL—REGARDS FROM ALL IN ROOM 307.

Miles Kington

"You'd think, for the amount we're paying in rates, they'd draw and quarter him as well."

LET ME OUT, I'M A PRISON VISITOR!

LORD LONGFORD reports on his rounds

"PRISONS," said the Governor to a sceptical audience, "Prisons, you may think, are a rotten answer. I couldn't agree with you more. You may prefer transportation, or humiliation in the public stocks, or flogging, or mutilation, or of course hanging. All these excellent ideas have been and in various parts of the world are still being tried. But if you are too squeamish, or high-minded to adopt any of them, you may be forced back on prisons as a reply to serious crime." I didn't and don't disagree with him.

That of course is not to argue that all or most of the people in prison to-day, chiefly men but some women, ought to be there at all. The sentences are too long and not getting shorter. Parole, the one real step forward in recent years, is administered in the most niggardly fashion, for which governments, not the Parole Board itself, must take all the responsibility. Thousands of people are held in prison awaiting trial who are not afterwards given a prison sentence. All sorts of sick persons are treated as criminals when they are really mental patients.

But in any foreseeable future under any conceivable degree of enlightenment, there will still be many people in prison. The instruction in Matthew XXV will remain as poignant as ever: "I was in prison and you came to me. Insomuch as you did it to one of my least brethren, you did it to Me."

There are in principle two good reasons for visiting prisoners, either individually or in the mass. One may seek to cheer them up, to make life seem worth living, and to provide some reason for self-improvement; or alternatively to investigate their conditions. The two purposes overlap. Twenty years ago, I undertook an inquiry for the Nuffield Foundation into the causes of crime, later published as a book. In the course of that Inquiry, I ranged up and down the prisons and Borstals of Great Britain, and learnt many things which were useful when I opened the first debate on prisons in the House of Lords in 1955. But at the same time I came to know a number of prisoners personally, which may have helped them and certainly educated me. With some of those prisoners I am still in touch. Some have made good, others have died in the meanwhile. In one case, my friendship led to a charge of homosexuality against me and the prisoner concerned. It was brought by a fellow-prisoner, who persuaded himself that I was obtaining illegitimate advantages for the prisoner in question. Two MPs of a Party other than mine posted off to Pentonville to receive his deposition and were, I gather, disgusted when there was nothing doing.

There are various ways of visiting a prisoner, most of which I have utilised. An official prison visitor, such as I was originally, before the war, in Oxford, talks to the prisoner in his cell, alone. Provided that one is not nervous, this is in theory the best method. Unfortunately one has to sign a document which restricts the area of conversation, and prison visitors in general feel inhibited from coming out into the open and exposing prison conditions.

A member of the House of Lords or the House of Commons enjoys certain facilities not available to the general public. For example, his visits do not count as part of the prisoner's very limited ration. On the other hand, a prison governor (male or female) sits in on the interview, which restricts the degree of intimacy established. These prison governors are usually as tactful and unobtrusive as possible. It is a real advance just lately that new regulations have been introduced and interviews are now held within sight, but not within hearing, of a prison officer. Talking to a prisoner about his or her soul, or even about one's own as part of the therapeutic process, is ludicrous with a third party sitting at one's elbow.

The great majority of citizens, most of them I suppose relatives, who visit prisoners go in neither as official prison visitors nor VIPs. I have made many such visits in the past. No experience is more poignant than waiting in a visitors' room, along with prisoners' wives and mothers. Many of them have made heavy sacrifices to be present. One feels abashed in the presence of their devotion.

But to-day my information must be derived from others. I am for instance President and one of the founders of the New Bridge for ex-Prisoners. Our representatives enter many prisons to make arrangements in advance for the prisoners' freedom. Conditions, we have discovered, vary enormously. In a place like Brixton, for example, stuffed to overflowing with prisoners on remand, a visitor may find himself talking to a prisoner with other visitors and prisoners cheek by jowl all around him. I gather things are not much better in

Wandsworth. In newer prisons like Blundeston and also Chelmsford, the facilities are quite impressive, with playrooms specially designed for children brought on the visit.

This last point brings one on to the strongest grievance—the severe limitation on the number of visits and the time allotted (one a month, in principle, and half an hour, except at week-ends). Here again, practice varies, but if we really believe that prisons are supposed to play any reforming role, the number of visits permitted ought to be doubled and then doubled again. And so ought the time allotted. Of course this will cost more money, but we have got to make up our minds once and for all that the amount of resources, human and material, that we devote to the prison service is absurdly, indeed shamefully, small. It is difficult to be up-to-date with figures here. Two years ago, I pointed out that we spent rather more than £50 millions a year on prisons as compared with something like £3,000 millions each on Defence, Education and Health every year. I should doubt whether the proportions now are much different.

When you hear this kind of question argued in the Cabinet, you realise that the Home Secretary asking for more money for prisons is facing a colossal prejudice. "Why should we spend it on them . . . ?" is asked all too readily. Politicians are aware or think they are, that there are no votes in Penal Reform, and they rationalise their prejudices all too easily.

Any public-spirited citizen ought to visit prisons partly to equip himself to recommend radical alternatives, partly to encourage the fellow human beings whose misbehaviour has landed them there, partly to remind himself of his own disposition towards weakness and wickedness. In the words of *The Imitation of Christ:* "Thou shalt count all men frail, but no man frailer than thyself." A prison is a good location in which to re-learn that lesson.

It is all too easy to enjoy visiting a prisoner, providing that he is fairly accessible and that one is not closely involved with him. The real test is whether one is prepared to go on helping him when he comes out. If Latin is still permitted in *Punch:* "Hic labor, hoc opus est."

A Lady is helping the Police with their enquiries

With Winifred Taylor, the first woman detective at Scotland Yard, the field is now wide open. At least, for BILL TIDY

"No thank you, madam. Not while I'm on duty."

"Sergeant Briscoe wants a little chat with you, Fierelli."

"Come out, Ridley—no thanks—you haven't got a chance!"

"I hate rotten stinkin' lousy coppers."

"Blimey, Super, info on the Midland Bank job's worth more than rissoles and chips!"

"Oh dear. Claudio's having an awful time deciding where to fit the truncheon."

If You Want to Know the Time, Ask a Solicitor

How far, ponders ALAN COREN, has police corruption spread?

EVENING all! We've got a saying up at Dock Green that One Thing Leads To Another. People, well, people come in all shapes and sizes, and it takes all sorts to make the world go round, but those of us who know that many a mickle makes a muckle, well, we're in a pretty good position to see how one thing leads to another, though, of course, least said soonest mended. Take old Mrs. Cublington, for instance: she's a dear old biddy, likes her tipple of course, but then what pensioner doesn't, I always say, live and let live and we're not long for this world, when all's said and done, and her arthritis has been giving her terrible trouble lately, well, all of us has his cross to bear through this vale of tears, I don't mind telling you, so, anyway, old Mrs. Cublington dropped into the Station the other night, and she was looking a bit more worried than usual . . .

"Hallo, Mrs. Cublington, and what can we do for you this evening?"

"Well, Sergeant Dixon, it's my dog Timmy."

"Run away again has he, then?"

"Yes, he's only a mongrel of course . . . "

"They're the best kind, Mrs. C, I always say."

" . . . well, I turned round, and he was gone!"

"Well, that's the way of this old world, Mrs. C, one minute you're there, the next, well . . . "

"I was wondering if you could keep an eye out for him."

"Glad to, Mrs. C, glad to. What are we on this old earth for if not to help one another? That'll be two pounds, in advance if you don't mind."

"But it was only a pound last time, and what with my old age pension not going as far as it used to and . . . "

"How'd you like a kick in the mouth, Mrs. C?"

"Well, no, Sergeant, I wouldn't like that at all, in cash was it?"
"Used notes, if you don't mind, Mrs. C, thank you very much."
"Good night, Sergeant."
"Good night, Mrs. C."

Well, it's a funny thing, coincidence, but just a night or two later, I was called to a burglary by PC Walker on his two-way radio. He wanted someone to hold the ladder and keep a general look-out and have the minivan ticking over, so I nipped round to 14 Mafeking Villas—we knew the owners were away, on account of they'd asked us to keep an eye on the place while they were in Torremolinos—and I was just helping PC Walker load his sack into the van when all of a sudden there was this terrible loud barking! I turned round, and would you believe it, there was Mrs. Cublington's little dog Timmy!

"Bloody hell!" says PC Walker, "That dog'll wake up half the street!"

"Poor little thing," I say, "he's prob'ly starving."

So I fetched him one over the head with my truncheon. I've always been very good with dogs.

But it was too late. The lights went on in the house opposite, and before I knew it, a large householder in a dressing-gown and poker was running across the road towards us. You know, people today have a fine sense of what you might call civic responsibility; your average Englishman doesn't just stand by, he's always ready to have a go, and he doesn't give a darn about the risk involved. It makes you proud to be an Englishman. I was just debating whether to kick him in the groin or put a quick half-nelson on him and ram his head against the side of the van, when a thought struck me.

"Quick, PC Walker, take your helmet off!"

As he did so, I grabbed his arm and twisted it up behind his back, just in time. The householder saw me, and stopped.

"Thank goodness you were on the spot, officer!" he cries.

I touched my helmet with my free hand.

"Always on the alert, sir," I say. "Caught this one red-handed. Here's one villain who won't be troubling us for a nice long time. In the van, my lad!"

We drove off, leaving the householder to recommend me for promotion, and as we were proceeding up the High Street in an orderly fashion, PC Walker let out a sigh of relief.

"Bloody quick thinking, Sarge," he says. "I don't know where we would've been without you."

"What's this we business?" I reply. "Got you with the stuff on you, didn't I? Shan't see you for a few years, my lad! Nothing the public hates more than a bent copper."

"But, Sarge, you were in on it from the start, it was me what tipped you off in the first . . . "

"You're not helping your case, Sonny Jim," I say, wondering whether I ought to punch him in the ear, for form's sake. "You go making filthy allegations like that, the judge is going to recommend a minimum PD!"

"What about half the swag, Sarge?"

"Bribing a police officer? Conspiring to subvert the course of justice? Tut, tut! Now, if I were to drop off at my house and leave the takings there, we wouldn't have no evidence, would we?"

"*All* the swag, Sarge?"

"You know, Constable, it's a fine life in the Metropolitan Police these days, isn't it? Starting salary of twelve hundred pounds, plus uniform allowance, London allowance, free accommodation, well, a single copper has plenty of money left over at the end of the week, wouldn't you say? Enough to spread a little of it around, say three notes?"

"*Every* week, Sarge?"

"Well, thank you, PC Walker! What a generous offer! Now, put your helmet back on, lad. One thing I hate is to see a nice young copper like you sloppily dressed."

You know, it's a funny thing, I don't know what put this into my mind, but a day or two later I had to call on Glass-Eye Charlie Swine, boss of the Lewisham Mob, in the line of duty. I was seconded to CID that day, on account of my son-in-law, Det. Sgt. Andy Crawford, was off on a child-molesting case, and CID were a bit short-staffed. So, as soon as I saw Andy go off in his dirty raincoat with his packet of boiled sweets, I put myself forward for plain-clothes duty. There were three of us in the Jaguar, and we'd taken the precaution of drawing three .45 Webleys from Stores, just in case the Lewisham Mob were unarmed—a revolver in good nick fetches anything up to fifty quid these days— and when we pulled up outside Charlie's club, he was there to meet us. He looked worried.

"For Gawd's sake!" he cries, "Turn your bleeding blue light on, you'll get me a bad name! I'M HELPING 'EM WIV THEIR ENQUIRIES!" he screams to a couple of bruisers who've come out of the betting-shop opposite, and he falls down and holds his kidneys, and gives out a couple of very professional moans.

"Up you get, Charlie," I say. "Inside!"

They were all there, in the back room, very surprised to see us. I sat down on the edge of his desk, admiring the hand-tooled antique leather top with my jack-knife, and allowing an exquisite Ming vase to fall and shatter on the marble floor. Charlie sucked in his breath, but said nothing.

"Nice little protection racket you've got here, Charlie," I say. "We wouldn't like to see anything happen to it. Would we, gentlemen?"

My colleagues shook their heads. There's no finer esprit de corps anywhere, I always say, than in the Force.

"Wouldn't it be a pity, Charlie, after all your years of hard graft building up a clientele you could lean on for—what is it, Detective-Constable Breene?"

"Five grand a week."

"—for five grand a week, wouldn't it be a pity if all that had to come to an end, out of pure selfishness?"

"You wouldn't dare," says Charlie, very pale.

"Dare what? Accidents happen, Charlie. I mean, we in the Force do our best to stop them, but—what's that funny smell, Detective-Constable?"

Breene examined the label of his empty jerrycan.

"I can't be sure, of course, Sergeant, but something tells me it might be petrol."

"Petrol! Charles Swine, I have to tell you that we are treating this as a case of arson. Where's my matches?"

Well, that about wraps it up for this week. Everything turned out all right, you'll be glad to know: old Mrs. Cublington's dog turned up, floating in the Thames; young PC Walker turned over a new leaf, and was found floating in the Thames; and our old friend Glass-Eye Charlie Swine stepped out of the ashes of his establishment, determined never to go back to his old ways. He kept his promise, and next week I hope to be able to tell you all how we found him floating in the Thames. It just goes to show you that, whatever folks may say, there *is* always a policeman around when you want one!

So mind how you go.

The British Godfather

BILL TIDY's underworld connections

"You're a promising boy, Salvatore. I show you unfair preference and you blackmail me!"

"A soft job like this is nothing. On the outside I could get you a title."

"You've done Slegg Alley for nearly five years . . . How would you like a better pitch, mother?"

"And to think that the guy I'm forging had the Fifth Earl of Sandwich as patron . . ."

"He wants to be a ballet dancer, OK, but he starts at the bottom like I did, sticking up petrol stations!"

"It's a police trap, Salvatore . . . Marry into this family and there's 673 names off our kidnap list."

Keith Waterhouse Goes Looking for an Orgy . . .

I, CHARLES SEPTIMUS PARKIN of 23A Jubilee Mansions, Norwood, make this statement voluntarily in the presence of Detective-Sergeant William Cooney and PC Throstle of "E" Division. I am forty-three years old and a clerk in the employ of British Fat Products Ltd. I am married in name only. I do not wish to add to that.

I first became aware of the permissive society on or about September 5 1969. I remember the date because it is the birthday of my niece Avril, and I had bought her a Kooky-doll as a present. I do not know why the Kooky-doll is still in my possession, or why she was in the cistern cupboard. I cannot explain why she is wearing fish-net tights, see-through bra and a PVC mackintosh instead of the après-ski outfit depicted on her box. The Action Man produced by Det.-Sgt. Cooney from the cistern cupboard in my presence does not belong to me. I do not know why Action Man is wearing only his boots. The Polaroid camera is for the purpose of taking holiday snaps. The photograph which I ate before being cautioned by Det.-Sgt. Cooney was a holiday snap.

On or about September 5 1969 I read in a Sunday newspaper about a wife-swapping ring in Mauncey Road, Birmingham, together with an exposé of certain magazines "for swingers only," also photographs allegedly taken at a drag party in Leeds before the reporter made an excuse and left. It is not true that from that day on I became obsessed by the permissive society, although what I read was certainly an eye-opener. I did not suggest to my wife Noreen that we should engage in similar activities. The phrase, "Let's get some fun out of life while we're still young, or are you too frigid?" is not one that I would normally use. I did not place an advertisement in the *Swapper's Digest*. I have never heard of the *Swapper's Digest*.

I now recall that I did place an advertisement in the *Swapper's Digest*. The fifteen back numbers of this publication under the towels in the airing cupboard are for my own use. The advertisement was a joke. It has been put to me that "Virile husband-and-wife duo wish to meet AC-DC couples, no prudes" does not sound like a joke, but I do not agree. It was an exercise in parody. I know nothing about an accommodation address in Soho. I received no replies to my advertisement.

I have never been in Mauncey Road, Birmingham.

I now recollect that I went to Mauncey Road, Birmingham, on September 9 and spoke to a woman now known to me as WPC Hawkins. My purpose in journeying to Birmingham was to visit an old army friend, 586 Cadger McNally, whose address I cannot at present remember. I asked WPC Hawkins to direct me to New Street Station. I did not employ any words such as "Are you a swinger?" I recall employing the phrase, "Where is the action?" This is an idiomatic expression indicating that I was looking for New Street Station.

I did not deposit a suitcase in the left-luggage office at New Street Station. I identify a suitcase produced by Det.-Sgt. Cooney as my property. I confirm that it did not fly to Birmingham of its own volition. The mask, riding-crop and length of rope are all my property. I purchased the mask at a novelty shop in Paddington in case my friend 586 Cadger McNally was giving his annual fancy-dress party. The riding-crop was a present for my married niece June, who is a keen horsewoman. I have no recollection whatsoever of proposing to my married niece June that I should be her gee-gee and that she should ride me around her living room. The length of rope was in case of fire. I have always carried a length of rope in case of fire ever since reading that Hans Christian Andersen did likewise. It has been put to me that Hans Christian Andersen is the same "Fancy-pants" Andersen who is now doing bird at the Scrubs for thieving lingerie off of clothes lines. To the best of my knowledge Hans Christian Andersen was a writer of fairy tales. I have been informed what the expression "fairy" means in common parlance. I have never been that way inclined. I have never been to Hampstead Heath.

It is not true that I was wandering about Leeds in a polka-dot dress and steel-blue nylon stockings on the night of September 9–10. The polka-dot dress produced by Det.-Sgt. Cooney was purchased at Selfridge's for my friend 586 Cadger McNally's fancy-dress party. I regard flushing clothes down the lavatory as a normal method of disposing of unwanted property.

Having been shown certain photographs, I now wish to correct any suggestion I may have made that I was not wandering about Leeds on the night of September 9–10, but I deny that I was looking for a so-called drag party. I was in Leeds for the simple reason that I got on the wrong train at Birmingham New Street Station. I was suffering from flu and had taken some tablets shortly before drinking a glass of beer. This must have made me light-headed. I was definitely not wearing the polka-dot dress, except for a short period.

I admit to having knocked at a door in Victoria Hospital Avenue, Leeds, between 12.30 and 12.45 am. I deny asking the lady now known to me as Mrs. Jeanette Henderson if there was room for one more. I deny suggesting to Mrs. Henderson that nobody would take her for a sailor. My purpose in knocking at the door was to ask for a glass of water. I was not wearing the polka-dot dress. I had recently drunk a carton of milk which must have splashed over my overcoat, giving it a polka-dot effect. I did not raise my overcoat to thigh level while in conversation with Mrs. Henderson.

Having been given an opportunity to reconsider that portion of my statement relating to the *Swapper's Digest,* I now believe that there may have been one or two replies to my advertisement. There may have been 1,753 replies. Certain parcels which Det.-Sgt. Cooney removed from under the floorboards in my presence may contain replies to my advertisement. I have not read any of them. I do not recognise a typewritten manuscript entitled *Kitty's Awakening*. I do not know of any invitation to attend a party in Tulse Hill for sex fun.

I am familiar with Tulse Hill. I may have been there on the evening of December 18. An important invoice had blown out of my office window on that day and I thought it might have landed in Tulse Hill. I may have been wearing a shortie nightdress under my raincoat. I often wear a shortie nightdress in the privacy of my own home as I understand there is no law against it. I wear it because it is convenient. At approximately 10 pm, on the evening of December 18, I remembered that I had not taken the dog for his usual walk. I put on a raincoat over my shortie nightdress and took him as far as the pillar box. The dog having slipped his lead and been run over by a coal-lorry I thought that rather than waste my outing I would proceed to Tulse Hill and look for the invoice.

I may have approached several householders in the Tulse Hill district with the words, "Have you a French kitten for sale?" I was not aware that this was a password. Owing to the accident to my dog I was anxious to obtain a new pet as quickly as possible. I do not know why I asked for a French kitten. I now think that I may have asked for a *fresh* kitten, meaning one that was only a few days old.

After a conversation with my wife Noreen I now recall that I have never owned a dog. I have been taking pills for a severe migraine and these, swallowed in conjunction with beer or wine, sometimes induce a sensation of owning a dog.

I deny hailing a taxi at Tulse Hill Station at 1.43 on the morning of December 19.

Having been assured that nobody is going to get their collar felt for taking a cab, I now remember hailing a taxi at Tulse Hill Station, but deny asking the driver if he knew anything about blue movies.

The taxi took me to my home. I deny saying, "Well, here we are at Iceberg Manor." I deny offering the driver double fare to take me to Hampstead Heath.

Certain evidence having been shown to me, I admit to being on Hampstead Heath at 3.16 on the morning of December 19 and approaching the gentleman I now recognise as Detective-Sergeant Cooney. I regret having prevaricated about this matter, but I was of the impression that wearing false moustaches went out with Sexton Blake. I concur that if I had stuck to false moustaches instead of polka-dot dresses I would not be in the situation in which I now find myself.

I confirm that I mistook Det.-Sgt. Cooney for a sex maniac, and that I asked him for information about any lewd, filthy, degrading and obscene parties that might be going on in the vicinity. I agree that I falsely represented my wife Noreen as being available for sex fun in the event of Det.-Sgt Cooney being able to assist me in my depraved endeavours. I now understand that my use of the words "sizzling," "versatile" and "hot pants" in respect of my wife Noreen was an offence under the Trades Descriptions Act, and I wish to express my regret for any embarrassment, distress and disappointment caused both to my wife and to Det.-Sgt. Cooney.

"Come on out, O'Mulligan, we know you're in there!"

Wishing This Enterprise Every Success

THE ALLIED PLASTICFOUNDERS & RUBBERWORKERS UNION

SPECIAL

Anyone having difficulty in obtaining copies of PORNOGRAPHY: THE LONGFORD REPORT should write without delay to The Connoisseur Bookshop, Greek Street, London, W.1. But hurry! Even our enormous stocks will not last long in the present fantastic demand! N.B. Anyone wishing for enormous stocks of their own should write immediately to The Connoisseur Bondage Co., Greek Street, London, W.1.
Please state inside leg measurement with order.

Atop London's famed skyscraping edifice of successful dirty books stands the wonderful glistening new dome of PORNOGRAPHY: THE LONGFORD REPORT. (Out tomorrow.)

Shimmering white, like a Dayglo sepulchre, this magnificent new all-British venture promises to herald a new era in commercial naughtiness: Kinsey, one of the earliest pioneers in the field, came close, David Reuben came closer, but not until PORNOGRAPHY: THE LONGFORD REPORT (60p at all good bookshops—and that's the point—) did the world receive its first Dirty Book It's Respectable To Read!

Today, as they showed me round the fabulous new enterprise, publishers Hodder and Stoughton were beside themselves (Hodder on the left, Stoughton on the right). "We're doing a first print of 100,000!" they cried, jumping up and down in

ILSE, BRITT, TALL SADIE AND ALL AT LOWER BELL, TOP FLAT, 14 CURZON MEWS, W.1.

Wish The Longford Report every success, and trust it drives sex out of the bookshops and back where it belongs.

24-HOUR SERVICE. PARTIES CATERED FOR.

FEATURE

selfless devotion to their craft. "This will make Virgin Swedes A-Go-Go and Take Me, I'm Ghanaian! and all their cheap, poorly produced, badly distributed kind look like the amateur low-profit rubbish they are. PORNOGRAPHY: THE LONGFORD REPORT ($1.95 in Australia and New Zealand, R1.70 in South Africa, $2.50 in Canada) is, perhaps, a small step for man," here they blushed modestly, "but a great step for mankind."

As we made our way through the splendid structure, all manner of famous experts on sexual mores and public opinion rushed to greet us, people like Professor Agnes Headlam-Morley, the Historical Adviser to the Foreign Office, Sir Frederick Catherwood, the former Director-General of the National Economic Development Council, Cliff Richard, famous Eurovision Song Contest runner-up, Peregrine Worsthorne, the typist, and Jimmy Savile, intellectual nonpareil and TV smoker. I glowed within at the knowledge that such massed expertise had been brought to bear on an issue which touches each and every one of us, if we're not careful.

I became convinced, as if one were to need such assurance, that the only thing which motivated the setting-up of this wonderful institution, PORNOGRAPHY: THE LONGFORD REPORT (weighs less than a pound, yet contains several hundred spotless pages, including eye-catching cover to ensure easy bookstand recognition), was good old-fashioned, pure and simple *(contd. p8)*

MR MALCOLM MUGGERIDGE WISHES TO ANNOUNCE THAT HE HAS MOVED TO NEW PREMISES. AGAIN.

The new premises are:
1) All sex is good for you
2) God is a turtle
3) The world sits on His back
4) I am Joanna Southcott

Any pop singer, peer, churchman, ringmaster, manufacturer of novelty rainwear, programme planner, or turtle wishing to associate himself with any of the above should write to Box 4088, where he will undoubtedly learn something to his advantage.

CONGRATULATIONS, CLIFF!
FROM THE TEAM THAT SHOCKED LORD LONGFORD!

THE COPENHAGEN CHAMBER OF COMMERCE
Takes Pleasure In Almost Anything

Ideal For Conferences, Bracing For The Elderly, English Specialities!
You read the book, you saw the movie, now meet the Shetland pony!

KINGSLEY AMIS ENTERPRISES

Suppliers of Bespoke Opinions to the trade, also wide range of ready-to-mouth clichés, manufacturers of articles, reviews, light verse, heavy prose, long boring fillers etc.

WISH THIS FUNCTION EVERY SUCCESS

Let Us Quote You (We Shall Anyway)

Zoo-Cars

R. G. G. PRICE

"Thieves who stole a pair of golden eagles and two snowy owls from Zurich Zoo may have been part of an international syndicate specialising in animal thefts, said a Zoo spokesman." *The Times.*

HE had been sweating it out for fourteen hours under the harsh lights, with the rancid cop-smell in his nostrils and the sickening fear of what was waiting for him if he cracked. He remembered Little Vlach, who had grassed on the Leeds yak job and ended in a quiet Esher bathroom with the bath full of piranha and the stereo belting out Ludwig Koch tapes to swamp the screams.

Harper of the Fauna Squad took another swill of congealed coffee and rasped the jagged rim of the iron mug against his unshaven chin. He hadn't had his clothes off since the news broke that the bison-house at Sir Edgar Heimer's private zoo, despite its world-famous security, had been broached and the irreplaceable herd filched.

Sir Edgar was a powerful, vindictive man. If the Superintendent's predecessor had been broken for letting the Syndicate move a pride of lions from Whipsnade to the Marseilles waterfront, what might not happen to him? In a dust-choked snarl, he began again, "How did you get the forklift truck onto the roof?"

"I wasn't there," Stalker repeated dully. "You know me, Mr Harper. I'm just a little guy, a pet-shop lifter. I always get picked up, don't I? I have my false coat-linings full of tortoises and the clinking gives me away."

"You've been working with the Syndicate for months," shouted Harper. "I'm going to get you for the Pont Street wart-hogs job, the Guards mascot job and the Old Compton Street cobra job. But first I'm going to nail you for this one. How long did it take you to get through the roof?"

Stalker didn't answer. Maltese Peony had grassed about the pandas that the Belleview Boys had salted away in Swiss Zoos before they did their stretch. Ants, they had used on her, just little, busy ants. They had nicked them from a public park in the tropics and smuggled them across inside jumping beans.

"Throw him back in his cell and spread the word that he's been more than helpful," said Harper with a cruel grin.

Momentarily, Stalker fell for the old routine. "Don't tell the Lean Man," he croaked, then what he had done hit him. He remembered that Hagman had ended alone in a Pinner basement with a vampire bat for inadvertently putting fuzz wise to some Sicilian boys who specialised in giraffe work.

"Tell me about the Lean Man," the Super purred.

Meanwhile, in his Operations Room, the Lean Man himself was examining the scale model of the streets near the London Zoo. Italian Mac was reading the timetable for the night. He was proud of his timetables. If they had a fault, it was never allowing for other traffic.

"Is the tunnel going to be big enough?" the Lean Man asked.

"We don't want the dromedary to stick."

"I worked out the dimensions across the railings with my theodolite," said Grifter, the Syndicate's technical man. "It was a bit difficult, triangulating without making the other visitors suspicious, but I managed it under my coat. I don't know about growth-rate. I've simply allowed five per cent."

"If the drom sticks, it's you for Lily," said the Lean Man with a genial grin. Grifter remembered watching the croc deal with a squealer. She was a slow eater, but thorough.

A call came through from the taxidermist. The replacement would be ready on time and should allay suspicion till dawn.

As the previous robbery had been via the roof, Zoo Security was now concentrating on roofs and they did not have to worry that anyone would be listening for tunnellers. All seemed to be going like clockwork. Only the Lean Man seemed worried.

News had come through the grapevine that the Chessington Mob were planning to hijack the loot on its way to the fence. A keeper in the Mob's pay would radio the route to be taken by the Syndicate's horsebox to the secret airfield. (Its elaborate equipment included gangways that could be adapted to anything from hippo to anaconda.) There would be a fake police diversion, the horsebox would be directed into a farm, the loot would be transferred and far up an Essex creek there would be a rendezvous with a submarine which would rush the precious cargo to a Californian collector who had tired of Tintorettos and craved new sensations. The operation would have to be carried out fast; until the Mob knew the route, they couldn't begin leaning on a convenient farmer.

Time was getting short now for the Fauna Squad. Stalker would never settle for immunity from prosecution and a police guard. What guard could keep out malarial mosquitoes, Black Widows or scorpions? They could never hide him away; the Syndicate would snatch half the guard dogs in London to track him down.

At about the time that Harper was confessing defeat and the Lean Man was checking supplies of a herb guaranteed to keep dromedaries pressing ahead, there were three telephone calls to a sleek Surrey rectory. The first offered a dugong and two tapirs—payment in soiled notes and no questions asked. The second reported that a minor job had gone wrong. The task force had panicked and left an ant-eater behind without wiping off their prints. The last was an inside tip that there was to be a great detente conference in London to which the Russians, Americans and Chinese would be bringing gifts of rare beasts.

(What happened to the dromedary? Did the Chinese delegation arrive with empty cages? Did the financier recover his bison-holdings? Was the Lean Man on a diet? I have received a threatening call which appeared to be from a mynah and I dare not tell.)

"Oh, come now! Don't look so surprised! You must have seen lots of this kind of thing on the box."

The Larry Report

on the plan to let prisoners' wives in for the weekend

* 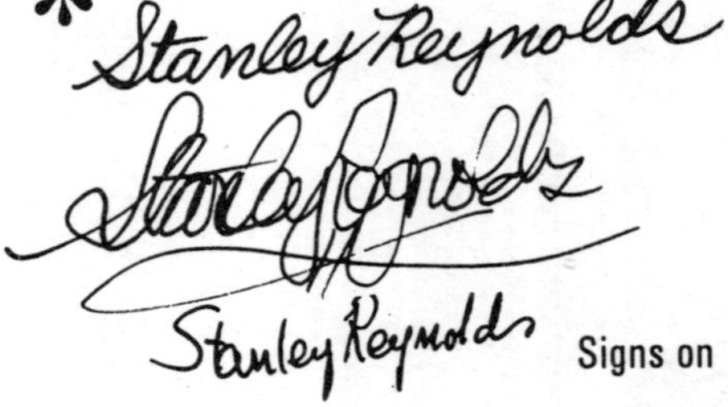

Signs on

Forging Ahead

OF course the greatest forging jobs right now are being done by the sex-change docs down dark alleys in Casablanca. Still, I'm glad to see that forgery, which is a nice old-fashioned sort of crime unlike polluting a river or a Ken Russell film of the life of a famous composer, is back in style.

First we had that attempt at forging the Prime Minister's signature. Admittedly this was rather a rough attempt, reminiscent, in fact, of the job I used to do on the old fellow's signature in spurious letters replying to various derogatory missives from headmasters complaining of my behaviour: *"Thanking you for yrs of the inst. to hand. The cheld Stanley has ben wrappremanded severeley and bodes for good behalfviour from this inst. on. (signed) A. H. Reynolds (Dad)."*

Another forgery to come to light was the counterfeiting of Baron de Rothschild's signature on a cheque by a Venezuelan wine-lover in Venezuela, which is by far the best place for a Venezuelan wine-lover to hang out. In fact, he was a French wine-lover or to put it more accurately: there was this drunk in Venezuela who took to reading the labels on the plonk bottles like we read the corn flakes packets—that was how bad this guy was, Mouton Rothschild claret for breakfast—and he noticed that elegant signature which the Baron has on his labels and so he wrote it on a cheque.

Fortunately for the Rothschild wine business the phoney signature was spotted. It seems the Baron has two signatures. One for cheques and another for on the bottle. Up to last week when I read this story I had not realised that Baron Rothschild and I had anything in common, but it just so happens that I have two signatures, one for ordinary days and another for when I'm on the bottle, which causes a great deal of head-scratching down at Barclays Sefton Park, Liverpool, branch when my

* Stanley Reynolds is currently helping graphologists with their enquiries.

cheques start bouncing in.

(One of my problems is that when I get a few jars of the Parsnip Cadet down I rather start bragging that I am ambidextrous, rather like some chaps start blowing about having been with the Desert Rats, and my left-handed signature is not too hot. "You signed this with your left hand, eh?" the fellow at the bank said. "Did you hurt your right hand?" "Not exactly, it was just more of my old trouble with my right elbow. Desert Rats, you know. Some kind of rats anyway, spiders and snakes, too.")

Where was I? Oh, yes, no sooner had these cases of forgery made the news than along came yet another counterfeiting yarn. This time from Liverpool (nothing to do with me, constable, I was curled up in bed at the time reading a good claret label). In Liverpool, it seems, they went one devious step beyond the normal practice of forging FA Cup Final tickets and this year started forging the voucher applications for tickets.

This came about when Liverpool FC issued vouchers to fans in a sort of raffle. People with vouchers with serial numbers ending in 4 could than apply for a Cup Final ticket.

This, of course, is nothing like running up fivers in the attic but it does show us that there still is a lively interest and a certain amount of expertise in forgery knocking about. And, given the enormous rise in crude crimes of violence, I think it is something to be encouraged with, if not an Arts Council grant, at least a cushy job in the prison print works, which is, I'll bet, where they learned the craft in the first place.

Actually the public has a warm spot in its heart for forgers. They are not toffs like high-class jewel robbers (as opposed to low-class jewel robbers) who get played by Cary Grant in the movies, but in the favourite crimes stakes, forgers and counterfeiters are only pipped at the post by jewel thieves. And, then, there are exceptions like that fellow who could turn out Old Masters. That was the chap who sold the bogus masterpieces to the Germans during the war and was only caught much later on after the war when they tossed science into the ring against him.

No jewel thief was ever so well loved, perhaps because the man who can turn out a Van Gogh or Rembrandt is fooling the art experts. Thus, the philistine in all of us is overjoyed.

One of the best stories of this kind came out only the other week when the experts at the Louvre in Paris, France (as opposed to the Louvre Bar & Grill in Paris, Michigan) spotted a number of phonies in Pablo Picasso's private collection. Here was Picasso going around painting three-eyed women and pictures of horses that even I wouldn't bet on and convincing everyone that it is great art and all the time he, himself, is buying duff paintings.

For a long time now counterfeiters have been merely a romantic dream of the past. Like ship-wrecked couples on desert islands, they dwelled only in the cartoonists' longing for a more leisured and stable time. The jet aircraft and the floating pound have relegated such stuff to the realms of fantasy.

In the great days of forgery, that is, when they actually used to make movies about them, it always took a tremendous amount of organisation, artistic skill, and sheer hard work to produce—what?—half a million in dud fivers. Nowadays you could overthrow a middle-sized Latin American republic with half the effort.

Just what has happened to the counterfeiters themselves I don't know. I suppose the sort of fellows who used to play Mr. Big, the brains behind the gang, have gone into asset stripping or running Arts Council supported Left-wing revolutionary theatre companies. But what about the old bloke in the eye shade, the mad prof who could 'ave bin a regular Rembrandt if 'e 'adn't bin bent? What's happened to him?

These old fellows with the eye shades always possessed beautiful daughters as well as the ability to engrave perfect likenesses of George Washington or Britainnia. These beautiful daughters always fell in love with the federal agent or the 'tec who tracked the gang down to the basement of the Chinese laundry in No. 10, The Wapping, and they explained the Dad's life of crime saying, "Father could have been a great artist but when he designed the Design Centre Award winning label for Super Alkleen and young Jeff Alkleen, old Herkermore Alkleen's son—and golly, to think I was engaged to Jeff (shudder) at the time—took all the credit, gosh, Dad just went I don't know. Kinda crazy in the head." "Never mind, Maria Concepta," the jut-jawed hero used to say, "we all go kinda crazy sometime, as a matter of fac' I'm kinda sorta crazy outta my head over you right now."

Well, they don't make pictures like that anymore. They don't make daughters like that either, come to that. Maybe that's the reason for the current lack of fellows running up fivers in back parlours. Maybe it was in actual fact these dopey daughters who drove them to it. I know they used to drive me to eating a lot of popcorn.

The instability of currency, the world's paper shortage, and the profits to be had making phoney French labels for cheap Algerian wine have probably all contributed to the demise of the traditional manufacturer of funny money. They have also not really taught anybody how to spell in the schools for the last 20 years and there is nothing like a few mis-spelled words on a banknote to start making Scotland Yard suspicious. At least, some of the old-time coppers.

"Where's the Fire?"

***BILL TIDY** joins the motorbike patrol*

"My wife's nearly due too, but you don't find me doing 110 down the bypass!"

"Calm down, lad. I just want to know where I can pick up some more of those smashing studs."

"C'mon, buddy, in the States we usually settle a little thing like this with a five dollar bill in the driving licence."

"Sorry lads, but he went through a red light and three pubs without stopping."

"I dunno how he gets away with it. He says he's a Russian spy and they run away screaming!"

I Must Ask You to Accompany Me to Euston Station

MILES KINGTON meets the British Transport Police

"THOUSANDS of people come in through Euston at 9 a.m. and think what a nice clean station it is. Fair enough. But I wish they could see it in the middle of the night."

The police office at Euston, after 11 on a Monday night. A comfortable Scottish sergeant called Jock, a veteran constable known as Trev, a plainclothes CID man with good looks and piercing eyes, a young constable with a constant smile. Any of them could have said that, and most of them did during the night. Except that they're far more real than anything in *Softly, Softly,* they could have been dreamt up for a TV serial, but their main concern with television is watching the closed circuit screens in the office. It's like seeing ten Andy Warhol programmes simultaneously. The Cafeteria. The Main Concourse. The Parcel Deck. The Booking Hall. A few shadowy figures slump over their luggage.

"It looks peaceful enough, but you never know when something's going to happen. Suddenly there's a punch-up, or a mysterious van arriving, and you have to radio one of our men out there."

The Cafeteria. The Booking Hall. The Concourse from another angle. Trev touches a knob and the camera zooms in on a man. He's just walking across with a case.

"That's our best camera. It's a beauty. German, unfortunately. Of course, if it's action you're after, you should come on a Saturday night."

Saturday night is football night. When Liverpool, Everton, Leeds, Manchester City, Manchester United, West Brom. are playing, they come via Euston. Hundreds of them. When they go back Arsenal, Chelsea and Spurs come to see them off. Hundreds of them, looking for action. All the police have got to keep them apart is five men. And a dog. Constables have been known to turn pale and vanish.

At that very moment the handler comes in with the dog. A furry, loveable Alsatian, very quiet and cuddly.

"Watch this," says Trev. He turns to the dog and says: "Chelsea!"

The dog suddenly turns savage, growls and strains at the leash.

"Mark you," says Trev fairly, "he does the same if you mention my name."

What do the police do beside watch TV and calm football supporters? Everything. Investigate ticket fraud. Examine pilfering. Fight the railway thief. Railway thief? Oh yes, it's a specialist career—they wouldn't touch a house or a shop, you know. They also have to deal with lost souls, homeless travellers, hard-core drunks, pickpockets, indecent exposers and railway rapists.

Last Saturday there were also routine incidents like three platelayers killed by a train, one suicide and a football supporter who leant too far out of a window and left half his head sticking to a bridge in Hitchin. It's not nice, but you don't expect niceness in the policeman's lot. Gilbert and Sullivan were absolutely right, was the first thing the Inspector said when he welcomed me.

"Time to go round the station," said CID at 1 a.m.

"You'll see our regulars," said Jock. "Mary Mitchell. Jock. Flynn. All of them. They live in the Gardens in the day and come in at night. Then we chase them out again. You've got to be a bona fide passenger to stay in Euston at night."

First stop, the luggage lockers. Most of them are big enough for a man to curl up inside, but for once they all seem empty of anything but luggage. Three or four sleepers on the floor are questioned for destination and left in peace.

"You've got to use your initiative on this job. If you haven't seen a certain face before, you give him the benefit of the doubt and let him have a one night stand. If it's a mother with child, say, with nowhere to go, you might discreetly show them a carriage which is going to be there all night and who's to care if you let them sleep there? If it's one of your hard-core winos from the Gardens, you talk them outside again. What's the point of arresting them? Even the dogs won't go near their breath. You'd have to take them in, loosen their clothing, remove their false teeth if any, lay them on a rubber mattress, observe them every half hour and at the end of it all find they'd only been given a day inside, after which they're back in the square again, while we are still defumigating the station."

Second stop, gents' lavatory. Squint under the doors for sleepers. Here's Jock, regular customer. You might expect them to bundle him out unceremoniously, but no.

"Come on Jock, wakey wakey. Up you get. Don't fall over—I hate the sight of blood."

"All right, I'm coming."

"Jock, you shouldn't do it," says his sergeant namesake. "Why do you drink that stuff?"

"I have to. I'm an alcoholic," he grins wildly.

"Hey, Jock, you've dropped your pen," says the CID and picks up a cheap biro from the floor.

In another cubicle, the young constable is talking softly to someone. Five minutes later he reappears. What was happening in there?

"Let's say that he resisted my attempts to wake him, so I left him in a deep slumber."

Second stop, ladies' lavatory, where the attendant is worried about a body on the floor. It turns out to be a young student lost for a sleeping place. Third stop, main hall, where a woman is sitting on her luggage.

"All right, love?"

"My husband's just left me."

They talk to her, promise to look out for him, to come back later and check how she is. A lot of the job is just that: talking. Using the accumulated practical psychology of a working lifetime to sort people out, and give each one advice, comfort, warning or firm pressure as it's needed. Out in the Gardens, where the bodies lie hopelessly under the trees, it's too late even for advice because here you're looking down the plug-hole of society. Another job for the police, because nobody else has to deal with them. Someone comes up to us. It's the missing husband, deciding to return. He's redirected and given hostel addresses.

The railway police are policemen, not railwaymen. Up on the parcel deck they even seem to feel slightly on enemy territory.

"The big problem here is pilfering. See this parcel? See the hole at the end? Five pairs of tights gone there. A pair of shoes gone here. This parcel is dresses, or it was, till hands got at it. All staff work."

Sometimes valuable-looking parcels get left in corners. Sometimes strange vans drive in, pick up the valuable-looking pile which has been just sort of left in the corner, and nip off again.

"See this trolley? Now if a good bloke spotted those packages lying off the beaten track like this . . . "

A good bloke?

"A good railway thief."

What's a bad railway thief, then?

"One that gets caught."

It's not the villains that arouse police animosity. Nor so much the football yobbos, or the layabouts, or even the press. It's the do-gooders for whom they reserve their special enmity, whether they are do-gooders in Parliament making life even harder for the police, or do-gooders passing by in the station who see the police driven to firm action and go away to complain about police brutality. The fall-out rate from the police is usually explained by inadequate wages in the papers; they explain it here in terms of a feeling that the dice are increasingly loaded against the police.

And yet they're cheerful and resilient. In the same breath they tell you that it's a mug's game and that they wouldn't have any other job. Perhaps as much as anything it's because they would hate to waste the inestimable experience they've won.

"When a constable is young and green, he makes all the mistakes. If he spots a wrong 'un in the waiting-room, he goes straight up and challenges him, and most likely earns a punch-up. What he should do is question the other people first, so the villain loses his confidence, not being able to feel he's being picked on. Or he stands over a trespasser with a stopwatch, when he should wander off for a few minutes giving him time to clear off. It's always the young constables who get assaulted, not the veterans."

"I'll tell you what experience is," says Trev. "If a young sprog sees a yob up to some villainy, he taps him on the shoulder and says 'Oy'. The villain runs, the constable follows and catches him after three hundred yards. Now, I can't run three hundred yards any more—can't run three—but what I *can* do, thanks to experience, is put myself in the right place so that when I say 'Oy', he turns and runs into my arms and I say 'Gotcher' ".

What do you learn from a night in Euston with the police? You learn that when a copper is forcing his way into a lavatory, it's not because he's a Fascist pig—it's because he's afraid there might be a dead body inside. You learn that there *is* a policeman there when you want one, and he's probably watching you on TV at that very moment. You learn that they are not saints—saints would make rotten policemen—but that they are not half as bitter or cynical as you or I would be. And you learn they'd like a little recognition in their own right as railway police.

"Anyway, write a nice article about us," said Trev. "Otherwise you're liable to be picked up on Euston Station with a valuable parcel found under your arm and, hello, Mr. Kington, what's all this then?"

It was the only piece of police brutality I witnessed all night.

Fortress Suburbia

by GRAHAM

"How do I know you're not somebody ***pretending*** *to be the vicar?"*

"One night you'll get me out of bed and it really will be a burglar!"

"Just checking! Did you send a man round to read the gas meter?"

"Have you got a licence for that thing, madam?"

"Arthur's started on a moat."

"Just off for a stroll to the local."

"Sorry, Tom! I should've warned you about the trip-wire."

"Awfully sorry—a short circuit!"

Secure as Houses?

JONATHAN SALE on how to make the prevention fit the crime

MR. T. next door doesn't miss much. It was a wet winter's night when he rattled the knocker and gasped, "There's someone prowling round the gardens at the back." We went through the house and out of the back door.

"He had a torch," said Mr T., "and when I spotted him he was in the garden of Number 38" (that is, chez my other next-door neighbour). We looked out into the night. Either the prowler had gone, or his battery had run down.

This nocturnal saga, which explains why my house has enough anti-burglar gadgetry to outdo Fort Knox after a bomb warning, will be continued when my nerves have stopped jangling, as they will after the soothing application of financial figures. The gross earnings were £81·6 million for 1974, the latest calculated by the magazine *Security Gazette.* The industry in question is crime, and the figure is obtained by taking the amount of goods recovered (18·2 million pounds) from the amount stolen (99·8 million) to obtain the grand total of £81·6 million.

My own enquiries suggest that this does not take into account the very real outlay necessary for the criminal with a pride in his work, an outlay which cannot even be set against tax—rubber gloves, ladders, skeleton keys, getaway cars, striped jerseys and bags labelled "Swag". A further complication is that the £99·8 million does not include unreported theft (for obvious reasons) or over-generous taking of "perks". But quibbles aside, we have to accept that the profit is more than 20 per cent greater than the figure for the previous year, and reflects partly inflation and partly bigger thinking on the part of the professionals.

We walked up the garden. I courteously allowed Mr T., who is fighting fit, for a pensioner, to lead the way. "That light," he hissed, "in Number 38 wasn't on before!" He picked up a fork and held it in a sloping arms sort of way. I peered cautiously over the fence and down into the yard of Number 38. Sure enough, there was a light on in a downstairs room, and the sash window was at half-mast. If you were a burglar who had climbed in, I thought, you wouldn't want to waste your torch battery when going through the piggy-bank. You'd want the light on.

Crime prevention is yet another cost resulting from crime itself. Although Britain has yet to reach the state of the Philippines, where more money is spent on private guard services than on the police proper (I use the word "proper" loosely, since criminals there are commonly thought to play a straighter bat than the forces of law and order), we must be coming close to it, to judge by the expensive technology available.

At one end of the scale, a bullion house at night may well be silently patrolled by radar, ultrasonic scanners, automatic 999 systems, and an electronic blip that every few seconds checks the whole bag of tricks for malfunctioning (such as is caused by a pair of wirecutters) and raises merry hell if the circuits aren't just so. At the other end of the scale, there are "Binders for your copies of *Security Gazette*", to deter anyone wishing to misappropriate February 1969. In between, there are cases that in unauthorised hands give off orange smoke and 100 decibels, and, for the heavier load, a Hampshire firm will let you have an armoured, bullet-resistant van or a "Protective" ("Not bullet-resistant"—clearly the Trades Descriptions Act is taken seriously in Hampshire) vehicle.

Another essential is facilities for "vault storage", and, Lord knows, we all have to store our vaults somewhere, while the Portastor Security Unit takes in its locked maw all the gear needed on a building site, which makes it easy for the criminal with a low-loader to make off with the whole Unit, wheelbarrows and all. Uniforms Unlimited with their "Quality Uniforms at Competitive Prices" will be a familiar name to all those wishing to start their very own private armies, but you may have overlooked Perko, "the low priced invisible door closer", as opposed, no doubt, to Pinko, and as probably recommended by Larry Grayson. And for the security fanatic who wants to broaden his horizons, there is the "Security Study Tour of the United States". He might see how they deal with alarm bells over there, those effective devices for keeping neighbours awake and even bringing to the courts a few miscreants who knock them to fragments in the attempt to get a decent night's rest.

"It is quite possible," I explained, unconvincingly, "that the light has just been switched on by Mr and Mrs D., moving, as they are legally entitled to do, from the front of the house to the back. I'll just pop round to ring the front door bell, and then we'll know."

One way or the other, I thought, probably the other. I went back through our house—we live in a terrace—and out of the front door, stepping over the low wall to ring the bell in the darkened porch of Number 38. There was a pause while nobody came to answer it. The advantage of this was that I didn't come face to face with a man whose matching accessories (after the fact) were a mask and a sawn-off shotgun. The disadvantage was that Mr and Mrs D. did not appear, to show the whole thing was a false alarm. Something rustled near me, but it was only a pile of ivy in the porch.

I rejoined Mr T., still staking out the back of the suspected premises. Nobody had vaulted out of the window and slunk into the night. We deduced that whoever had opened the window and switched on the light was still there. Now was the time to take action on behalf of Mr and Mrs D., at whatever risk to life and limb.

"I'll go and phone the police," I said.

Some of the electronic hardware is liable to misuse. Why would anyone on the level want a machine that, according to the advertisement, "will record up to 40 telephone conversations simultaneously"? But there's nothing so dodgy about another form of communication, the closed-circuit television. There must be more of us British looking at each other via this device than there were looking at *We British* (at least, I hope so). There are versions that allow you to have under observation a caller at the door of your block of flats, and even, in the case of Telelock Ltd, allow you to relive the experience via the "permanent film record of callers". With these, you can make your own entertainment, greeting callers with "Hello, good evening and welcome to the John Smith Show, live from 45 Endersby Crescent, Cumbernauld. Perhaps you could tell viewers something about yourself? A tax collector, how fascinating. I'm sorry, we've got to take a break now, see you back on the show next month, possibly."

When it comes to factories, the closed-circuit systems are more elaborate, to such an extent that *Security Gazette* can write, "It is essential that a system of pan, tilt and zoom cameras with video tape-recorders is linked with a two-way radio installation." It's surprising that anyone who operates these replicas of BBC Television Centre doesn't have to belong to the union of studio technicians which blanks out screens from time to time. You may prefer to have a machine watch the monitor sets for you, in which case your best buy is Telesentry, "an advanced automatic motion detection television system designed for visual security" but not intelligible English. This wakes you up if one of its cameras is showing something moving (an intruder) or can't see as far as it once could (because of smoke), and should have implications for those who make their living from television criticism and wish to be alerted if anything of interest is transmitted.

It felt like ages before the police arrived, and it was in fact ages, since they couldn't find our road on the A–Z. *Finally, their flashing blue light, plainly visible as it raced feverishly up and down the nearby main road trying to pick up the scent, announced their arrival in our tiny street. I showed one of the uniformed policemen through the house and into the garden of Number 38, courteously allowing him to lead the way. Through a chink in the curtains of the room with the offending light I saw the most horrific sight of my life.*

Mr and Mrs D. were watching television.

At this point, Mr D., hearing us shuffling around outside, came charging out to see what gave. At this point, the policeman started to apprehend him. At this point, I pointed out that he was guilty only of being the inhabitant of the premises, and of being in possession of a door bell that did not function. At this point, the police said something about better safe than sorry, and goodnight.

With all the equipment available, you need someone to install and run it, and the growth of the security business is phenomenal. Securicor, for example, had only two lads in uniform (their own, that is) at the end of the last war, while today their staff in Britain alone totals 14,000 and their annual turnover is £40 million. While no one outside the criminal profession objects to the work done by that and other firms protecting places of work, it is the home that really concerns us, particularly at night when there's rather too much creaking of boards and rattling of windows to sleep soundly. Nobody wants to contribute to the upper income group of housebreakers (in the £20,000 p.a. bracket, according to *Hand-in-Hand,* the journal of the Commercial Union Insurance), or to the earnings of their more modest colleagues.

Although decent, "five-lever" locks are essential, they are not enough on their own. A man who worked in a family business of breakers and enterers once told me that he and his brothers, confronted by a door bristling with unpickable gadgets, noticed that its flimsy wood was susceptible to a few hefty shoulders. That's what I call lateral thinking. (Police are looking for a Mr de Bono, who they think may . . .) To save you wasting your money, and their time in taking down details after you have been burgled, the police will happily send round a crime prevention officer to case your joint and give free advice. My own advice, cheap for the price of this copy of the magazine, is that it's no good installing closed-circuit TV if you forget to close the downstairs windows when you go out. That is what I call straight thinking.

Next day Mr D. popped round about something else and happened to mention that he had been collecting ivy from his back garden the night before. With a torch. By the time we had worked out the implications of this, he had gone. Still, I took it as a warning; the next intruder may not be a figment of a neighbour's imagination, and I am now loaded with so many locks and bolts that I have to allow five minutes extra every morning to get out of the house. The second moral to be drawn from the true story is that you mustn't trust the figures for crimes known to the police during the period 1974/5 for the Metropolitan area. They are one too many.

Monet Makes the World Go Round

ALAN BRIEN's instant guide to the art thefts of the world

LAST year, according to a dispatch from Rome, 273 Italian churches and 27 museums were robbed of their art treasures. The latest raid, on a Milan gallery of modern art, raked in a haul of 28 paintings, including a Gauguin, a Renoir, a Van Gogh and a Cezanne. The reverberations of this new criminal fad reached here a few days later when Shaw Taylor of TV's *Police Five,* and Britain's premier grass, showed us black-and-white reproductions of some missing Old Masters, including a Raphael worth £3 million, and asked us to keep an eye open in pubs and street markets for anyone trying to flog tenth-hand canvases at suspiciously low prices, such as, presumably, £50 a square inch.

Italians are notorious for their inability to keep their hands to themselves, and a Renoir or a Rubens is probably irresistible to a nation of bottom-pinchers. But who do they expect to fence their loot? Only the rich can afford to make a bid, even at 10p in the pound cut-price offers, and they can only have two reasons for acquiring art objects fallen off the back of a lorry. Either as an investment—and who would respect the provenance of a work described as "formerly in the collection, for about 24 hours, of *Signor Grosso"*? Or as sign of status—and who can you trust to be shown the *Mona Lisa,* framed in brown paper in the cellar, by a custodian with a flashlight in one hand and a shotgun in the other, knowing that they may never leave the premises alive?

Even legitimately owned masterpieces are about as convenient to have around your house as the albatross was to have around the Ancient Mariner's neck. I once had dinner at the Garrick Club with half a dozen distinguished film-makers, men whose appreciation of the human condition was spoken of with hushed appreciation by regulars of all-night sessions at the National Film Theatre, only to find that the talk, as the candles guttered low, relentlessly stuck to the subject of what was the best burglar alarm to protect your collection.

Half of them confessed that they daren't inspect their own possessions without an appointment for fear of sparking off electric-eyes, seismic triggers, invisible trip wires and hidden foot-fall-activated microphones and bringing the local fuzz thundering down on their necks. Just a week ago I was invited by a diplomat to inspect his clandestine assemblage of paintings by Soviet dissident artists, smuggled out a risk of international incident. By mistake I arrived at the service entrance of his opulent penthouse, two luxury flats knocked together, exactly on time—only to hear his wife's voice quavering behind a door like the great gate of Kiev as though I might be the Boston Strangler. Even inside, we moved from room to room, her great ring of keys jangling as each was carefully unlocked and locked again, as though on a conducted tour of Castle Frankenstein.

In the world of art thefts, the rich have to protect themselves only against the rich. The rest of us could not afford to buy their missing treasures, however discounted. But even if we got them free, we would not have the money to protect them from visits by the illicit dealers.

My own taste runs to the sort of painting that almost nobody wants to bother to strap on the roof of the car as a gift, let alone run up to more than one figure at an auction. Sometimes they are not so much paintings, more like touched-up photographs, such as the genuine group portrait of the last Royal Family but one which now hangs over the cooker. A pair of Shirley Temple moppets, with blonde curls and blue eyes, masquerading as Princess Elizabeth and Princess Margaret Rose, a dark-haired, bobbed pearly-queen of a Queen, and a King George VI with the nobly wooden presence of a rocking horse. And I particularly appreciate, pointing it out to visitors, a corona of damp stains and fly specks which halo the group around.

I covet very much a classic tableau which covers half the wall of a friend of mine. There is a sense in which great paintings are very much alike, you've seen them before in 100 coffee-table books, and quite likely you've grown to prefer the colours in the reproductions. But a really terrible painting, equally all done by hand after all, is likely to be unique. The one I'm thinking of displays a lot of naked women in a kind of cave waiting for the visit of some legendary demi-god, carefully kept out of sight because the painter knows his limits, and one of his limits is that he can only paint women. Well, not exactly women, one woman to be precise, and then only in profile.

So that you have the spectacular, endlessly enjoyable view of one lumpish, ginger-haired creature, with drop-away chin and piggish tip-tilted nose, after another staring glumly to left or right. It is to be presumed that the painter had only one model available, somehow I think it must have been his landlady's daughter. And I know that she must have refused to take all her clothes off, because his knowledge of the female anatomy below the waist is curiously insecure. Every goddess, or whatever, possesses only one leg, which joins the torso at the pelvis and melds into the stomach, giving altogether the impression of a troupe of one-wheel cyclists in some third-rate road company, touring version of the Folies Bergères.

And yet, I have to confess that I greet this appalling travesty each time with delight, as I spot some new grotesquely comic distortion, which I cannot always summon up in the presence of the perfect correctness of great art. If someone would steal that for me, I'd pay the best price I could afford. One thing, nobody could mistake it for a print. It has to be the original.

I feel rather the same about furniture. I couldn't bear to fill the place with desks and tables and chairs and sofas which could only deteriorate from the moment I got them, under constant assaults by cats and children and drunken friends. When I buy something tenth-hand, I sit down to improve it—and change would be improvement—and when I'm finished it often looks, as my visitors often comment, almost as good as fifth-hand.

Not that I know anything about furniture restoring. I just use the materials at hand—a bottle of brandy, a jar of olive oil and a tub of Marmite. And I use this palette purely by instinct. The spirit removes excess of grease. The oil restores a gloss where other people's spirits have left scorched Rorscharch blots. The Marmite tones in scratches and chips. If you can't use my furniture, come the days of siege and famine you could always eat it. To turn a £3 sideboard into a £7 sideboard is probably the limit of my leger-de-main. But it gives me pleasure money couldn't buy—well, not under a tenner. And I'm never going to need a guard dog.

In Praise of Crime

HENRY CECIL

THERE is so much to be said in praise of crime that I find myself, like the bank-robber arrested by a Chief Constable, with an embarrassment of riches. Where would most of us be without crime? If there were no crime there would be no books or plays about crime. Look at the consternation among writers (and readers) of thrillers when Parliament abolished the death penalty. Half the suspense was gone. Some writers are reduced to saying "this took place in the days of the death penalty," but the public will not accept that for long. The joy of the thriller is that it really could happen. There are a few people who are satisfied with ghost stories or other fantasies. But most of us want to read about something which would be possible in real life. The successful thriller is the credible thriller. If no one robbed trains or banks, if wives no longer poisoned their husbands and husbands no longer drowned their wives in the bath, a substantial portion of modern literature would disappear. The abolition of the death penalty was indeed a serious blow for authors but it was not a deadly one. Messrs. Kray and Mr. Richardson (to refer to them as *The Times* would) showed that there is still enough going on in the criminal world to provide writers with ample material for an indefinite period.

Writers of fiction are deeply indebted to criminals. But where would writers of fact (and this includes some journalists) be without them? And how should we manage without the comforting headline BIG SNATCH IN PICCADILLY, which tells us at once that no war is imminent, no king has been dethroned, that butter has not doubled in price, and that there has been no devaluation of the pound and no increase of taxes or other disaster?

But this is only sounding the first introductory notes of the paean of praise. What about those whose lives are dedicated to crime and the criminals? If there were no crime it is true that the police would still have motorists to play with. But what about prison officers? They would be reduced to locking each other up in cells and then letting each other out again, if only to keep in practice. And the legal profession? Where would that be? It is an established fact that the increase in crime coupled with legal aid, has not only restored the falling fortunes of the Bar but has actually made it a profession which penniless students are anxious to join. No longer has the newly-called barrister the years of bread and water and waiting, when he can only console himself by telling his girl-friend stories of cases which he has seen *other* people conduct. How long did the newly-called barrister have to wait in the bad old days before the briefs started to arrive in sufficient numbers to enable him to pay for board and lodging? Three years, five years, ten? Today it is a mere six months before he is licensed to lose anyone's case for him and to make any number of speeches in mitigation on behalf of one or more of those public-spirited individuals who live by breaking the law. Or he can even suggest to the jury that they are actually not guilty. What should my client want to steal a bicycle for? He already has two. (Where did he get those?)

The judges could manage without crime. They would still be paid their salaries and could spend most of their time in court by tossing up imaginary coins to see who is to win in road accident cases. But what about the probation officers, the voluntary social workers and the earnest young people who want a Radical Alternative to Prison? It must give a good probation officer a considerable thrill when partly as the result of his help and advice he sees a man with many previous convictions doing a steady job, living with one wife and keeping out of trouble. But what thrill will it be when they all keep out of trouble? And what will the earnest young people do when there are no prisons to want Radical Alternatives to?

And think of the officials in the Home Office spurring on successive Home Secretaries to try and get more and more money out of the Treasury to build bigger and better prisons. For many of them it would be the end of the road. No new prisons, no new borstals! It's unthinkable.

And what about prison chaplains and prison visitors? Even Members of Parliament (who periodically shed tears when someone refers to the degrading practice of slopping out, still maintained in many prisons) would have to find some other evil to deplore and ignore.

And what about private security organisations? No more money to be escorted to banks, no more bejewelled old ladies to be protected, no more vans to be robbed in lay-bys.

And when you think of the amount of employment which crime gives to honest members of the public and the amount of entertainment which would be denied to us if there were no crime, it is a sombre thought that the people who get the least out of it are the criminals themselves. There are, of course, a few who make crime pay. They constitute a very small minority, but let us be thankful to them too. For they help to keep the whole movement alive. Without them some of the most interesting episodes in criminal history would never have occurred. They themselves make the best of both worlds. With no previous convictions they are eligible for election to many respectable bodies, they can even be parliamentary candidates and who knows if every now and then one of them may not slip into the legal profession? Fortunately he can never rise to the top of that profession. No highwayman has ever managed to get on to the Bench. It's as well for criminals that this has never happened, for sentences by criminals on criminals would be astronomical. To teach them an important lesson—not to be of good behaviour but not to be caught.

We need not worry about the future. Fortunately successive British Governments have realised for the reasons which I have mentioned and no doubt for others too that it is necessary in the interests of the nation that crime should go on. How otherwise can one explain their failure to take my advice and double the police force?

"You don't like mass break-outs! What sort of a fool do you think I feel, coming here on my own?"

"A petticoat crime wave is sweeping the world—and some experts blame Women's Lib

WOMEN FOR CRIME

AN UNDERGROUND NEWS SHEET

September 1976 Frank, Fearless, Frantic

Editorial

NED KELLY ALSO RAN

Roll on the "petticoat crime wave", as Fleet Street loves to call it.

Since that twee phrase was coined, we have seen Godmothers taking over throughout the Mafia. And yet there were people who thought that women could never rise above shoplifting!

As we write, two more "Sealink" ferries have been sunk in the English Channel by the Girton pirate, Mavis Rice-ffolliot. A pity Mavis had to decimate her mutinous crew afterwards. As we all know, she believes herself to be a reincarnation of the seventeenth-century Mary ffolliot, the Terror of the Antilles. We can't wait for the day when she finally succeeds in luring the scared Home Fleet from harbour!

Yes, sisters in crime, we're on our way. Who wants to be the "statutory woman" on a male-organised bank raid? Certainly not Bazooka Bess, whose all-woman gang narrowly missed the Concorde over Kew the other day. We all had a good laugh over her "WANTED" poster: "Frequents Women's Liberation gatherings, abortion rallies and radical assemblies of all kinds; a free contraception fighter; opposes marriage; bites nails; reads *Guardian*." Why, that would describe any or all of us!

Talking of "WANTED" posters, did you see the one they put out for Shirl Fury? "£50,000 Reward," it said. "Wanted For Cattle Rustling, Dockyard Arson, Attempted Genocide, Grand Larceny, Subornation of Juries, Champerty and Meter Thefts in Five Continents." Where's your Ned Kelly now? Did someone mention Charlie Peace?

ATTAGIRL, SHIRL!

HEROINES OF THE PAST—No 27

By "Priscilla"

IF YOU are a fan of the *Guinness Book of Records*—and who isn't?—you will know that the greatest bigamist of all time was Mrs Theresa Vaughan, who confessed in a Sheffield court in 1922 to taking part in 61 bigamous marriages in five years.

How do you view Theresa's "crime"? Is she to be honoured for making a laughing-stock of three-score males? Is she to be censured for going through the humbugging ceremony of marriage at all? Remember, Women's Lib had not then been invented and women's crime was still in its infancy. Remember also that marriage, if astutely entered upon, was a useful way of separating men from their wealth.

Wherever I hear Theresa Vaughan discussed, at dinner tables or in bus shelters, I find views are sharply divided. For the best postcard on Theresa's problem I will award a copy of the new coffee-table book *Great Hellcats of History*.

These women prisoners demonstrating, half-stripped, on the roof of an Italian gaol are demanding a swimming pool, air-conditioned cells, orgy facilities, holidays with pay, free *Asti Spumante*, a £50 bonus for every month served, pre-release film shows, free postal divorce, handsome male gaolers and absolution of sins from birth. Our comment: Wake up, Holloway!

Readers' Forum:

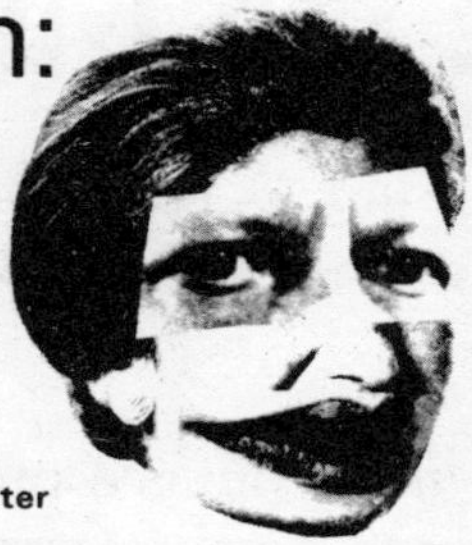

◀ **See letter**

Unfair to women?
AM I alone in resenting the vicious misrepresentations of wanted women by those responsible for putting out Identikit or Photofit pictures, not to mention "artists' impressions"?

Either these "likenesses" are the work of sexist creeps, or the eye-witnesses who passed on the descriptions were terrified out of their pathetic wits.

However, I suppose I should not be protesting, because if the police imagine I look like the Missing Link, as viewed by a Picasso disciple on an acid trip, I ought to be reasonably safe from arrest.

"LAUGHING BLUE EYES," Sidcup.

Probation Problem
NOT so long ago I was unlucky enough to be caught stealing men's underwear from clothes lines. Now my probation officer, Miss Golightly, is showing an unhealthy interest in me. This would not matter so much if I had not been invited to join an all-woman gun-running party in the Mediterranean. It is my chance to break into the big time, but Miss Golightly refuses to let me out of her sight. What can I do?

"ALL MIXED UP", Durham.

● *Tell your probation officer that her first duty is to her client. If she believes this, as so many of them do, she will not stand in the way of your happiness.*

Young Hopeful
IS it true that Chagalls are the easiest pictures to copy? My art teacher is an old stick-in-the-mud and refuses to give me a proper answer, but I want to start doing Chagalls now so as to buy a nice home for Mum and Dad.

Linda-Lou (aged eight)

● *Yes, dear, Chagalls are probably your best choice, but remember there is terrible competition. Have you thought of stealing pussy-cats for their furs?*

Born that Way
I SEE from the *Sun* there is a theory that women get drawn into crime because at an early age they associate with older men and are led astray by them. What arrogant nonsense! What typical male conceit!

When will the world see that we women are born with as great a natural capacity for crime as men? It is just that for centuries we have allowed our natural talents to be stifled. Let us have dishonour where dishonour is due!

I might add that, in the main, our backsides are better shaped than those of men for squeezing through fanlights.

Lucy Snuff, Wimbledon.

Careers for Women (12)

THE FENCE

THE TRADITIONAL image of a fence is of a shifty, dirty, middle-aged slob posing as a general dealer. When stolen goods are offered to him, he points out their defects, spits disgustedly on the floor and pays a twelfth of the real value. Every now and then he shops one of his clients to keep on the right side of the law.

This routine can be performed just as efficiently by a woman—except that she is unlikely to indulge in the disgusting habit of spitting on the floor.

To become a fence all you need is an entree to one or two Confederacies of Crime, as they are called. Deal only with honest thieves, not with hippies and similar rubbish who will only attract the attention of the authorities.

Stock a few lines of honest goods too. Very often you can make more money out of buying and selling the legitimate stuff than the hot stuff, and you may even be tempted to go straight. But hot deals are more fun!

Make your premises attractive with simple flower arrangements, but do not overdo it, or the police will suspect you of keeping a bawdy-house. If the sergeant says, "What's a nice woman like you doing in a dump like this?" wink broadly and say, "Trafficking in stolen goods." He will then laugh loudly and go away.

Next week: THE PIMP.

THE FIRST All-Ladies Lynch Gang is reported to be operating successfully in Alabama and has spread terror among male chauvinistic pigs throughout the lower Mississippi Basin . . . "Vitriol Vera" has escaped from prison in California and is looking for her 500th male victim . . . Eskimo Nell is alive and well and has collected a fine set of parking tickets at Thule, Greenland . . . The first woman ever to be charged in Britain with "Peeping Tom" offences has been admonished at Bradford, where the magistrate said, "I suppose you regard this as some sort of breakthrough for your sex" . . . A column of *carabinieri* was routed in the Pontine Marshes when it clashed with a demonstration in support of witches' rights . . . "Bronx Betty" has been successfully testing the 15 denier stocking mask up and down Fifth Avenue last week . . . Latest forecasts show that by 1980 Britain will contain as many gaols for women as for men.

Support our Advertisers!

CAT SUITS for Cat Burglars! In form-flattering Black, White, Marmalade or Tabby. Three lengths of tail—Long, Short and Manx. Neat swag pouch and padded *derrière*. Write for price list. Feline House, The Quadrant, Stoke-on-Trent.

Another male bastion falls! Three-card trick and thimble-rigging can be mastered easily by women. Learn by post from Madame Ramona—then clean up in race trains. Ramona Institute, Bray, Bucks.

First Steps in Treason. The home kit for the housewife. "It really rakes in the roubles"—Ethel P., Solihull. From all good underground bookshops.

We Name the Guilty Manual

Investigations indicate that this do-it-yourself detection article is the work of none other than LIBBY PURVES

HERE I am then, in these bungee plimsolls, with this night-glass; my raincoat reverses to startling tartan, I drop my head, splay my feet, I am unobtrusive. I have stood before a mirror saying Good Morning Madam, Goodness I Wish I Had Your Memory, Tall Man Then Was He? Stocky? . . . there is this pad, too, stapled inside my coat pocket for making secret notes. I will take it out in a minute, and scan it with my hard, hooded eyes.

It says LEIWTH YADRSP EL TSHIRT BLAFFT. In Arabic script. Ah well, so much for my on-the-spot notes; it was going to be a surprise, the first article to be written entirely inside a raincoat pocket. They could have put that in the advertising. But it seems I didn't read the bit about using a short pencil; long ones stick out and get involved in the lining and go arabic on you.

Not that I've *forgotten* a single detail of the whole ghastly business, anyway. My coat pocket may be a mass of inky oriental calligraphy but my psyche is scarred as legibly as you could wish. It started when I was proceeding through the small-ads of a weekly, and had my eye caught by the seductive offer of a Private Detection Instruction Manual by one ex-Inspector Meek. As the owner of a luminous skeleton, a flexible pocket saw (As Used By Nato Troops), and a vile set of collapsing cardboard shelves, I already belonged to the legion of idiots who know that to send off hopefully is better than to have it arrive; the King Kong pillowcase and the unbreakable (ho!) casserole bear enough witness to the sad futility of buying from an artist's impression, but the habit is not curable, and if I ever rise in the consumer scale it will only be to send off more and more money for reproduction Anglo-Saxon pocket sundials in solid silver £95·00, Sunday supplement sofas, and commemorative platinum medals in strictly limited editions.

At £2·75, the ex-Inspector's opus seemed cheap at the price for a new career; after all, in an age of professional uncertainty and articles everywhere about the Redundant Accountant who finds a new life as a market gardener, who can afford to ignore profitable new alleys? Sherlock, Sexton, Hercule and Lord Peter stood approvingly by the pillarbox, and my shoes grew noiseless and brisk as I walked away from it.

Private Enquiries began by reassuring me that I had a head start. CID detectives, it explained, have a minimum height requirement of five foot eight, and spend two years on the beat. Hence "the most incompetent thief can smell a detective from a very long way off by his height and by his built-in $2\frac{1}{2}$ mph plod." Strewth, sleuth, that means a five-foot-six woman with a built-in 1 mph shamble should prove an impenetrable cover. So cheered, I mastered the mnemonic number code for stolen vehicle (converted to letters, the *Punch* telephone number tends to read LOVE ME BUT BE PRUDENT); I practised scanning people's faces by looking over their shoulders, covered the kitchen in white powder to deduce that nobody was bothering to wipe their dabs, let alone their coffee, off the top of the fridge; and even took in my stride the author's gloomy announcement that "The Private Detective has no powers and is universally detested." I always wanted to be in a rat-pack anyway.

There are certain cultural gaps to be bridged, true; but eventually, the most literary of us may surely learn to refer to the quarry as "chummy" (as in "chummy was still at his tricks when I resumed the observation"); to think of missing persons in terms of *Ears obscured by hair, Nose small jewish, bow-legged, adenoids, Fond of going out with men.* Easy.

We could learn to suspect slow-moving, absent-looking citizens of secreting flat packets of supermarket bacon in the folds of their umbrellas. And mark down as a probable felon any suspect who tended to close his eyes during questioning. *Pretending to be dead or asleep is a defence mechanism older than the caveman,* so, reading on in a dozy trainful of fellow-men, I decided that the one fastest asleep would become my quarry when it came to practising Chapter 7, *Following and Watching*. He had a sheepskin coat on, and I scanned his Salient Features and mnemonicked them before returning to my studies.

But a chill began to creep over the research. Forgers I like, burglars, suave lovable master-criminals played by Peter Sellers; but certain casual insights into human society afforded by the ex-Inspector began to prove enough to leave any gathering of social-realistic novelists shaking their heads and knocking fag-ash into their Olivettis. *The older, sock-stealing class of male often smells of drink,* he mentions, opening up a new seam for popular sociologists; and then adds a quite unwanted dimension to history with the show-stopping observation *Between the wars, gangs of fearless middle-aged women used to raid the department stores and stuff the loot into bloomers of immense size and strength.* And it goes on.

Henry James and Jane Austen are swept out of business by the bald sentence, jammed in anyhow amongst the Pittsburgh wedding-day murders and insurance compensation: *Young females, aware of the value of a look of wide-eyed innocence, have been known to practise it before a mirror.* I had a girlfriend, young and female, who used to practise laughing silverily up and down the scale; but until then I'd forgotten it, never had to make that unwillingly acquired knowledge a part of my profession.

Your whole world vision gets knocked into sharper focus when you're a *PD*, as we PD's say; one great work of art at least will not look quite the same after reading that *Old Granny in her chair has been the custodian of housebreaking implements and coining gear from time immemorial;* I returned with nothing but a knowing sneer to my bedside copy of *Little Women* after discovering that *the bed is always a favourite place of concealment especially if the occupant is old or apparently sick.* Little Sick Beth probably had the whole family's jemmies down her nightie.

And as for the majesty and security of our great thoroughfares, Chapter Nine boredly informs the reader that "It used to be said that once in his lifetime every criminal in Europe walked along the Strand . . . a respectable proportion of murderers end up arrested for insulting behaviour in that thoroughfare." God, I *worked* there for a year, presumably surrounded by overwrought stranglers dropping their trousers at passing police cars; and yet I kept my innocence intact until I came to this businesslike exposé. We PD's have to stand, in these bungee plimsolls, looking over the shoulders of adenoidal missing persons and listening wearily to the phrasebook recital from each intercepted cheese-lifter. *Did I really officer, how silly of me! I am not well, just out of hospital, I thought I had paid, my little boy/girl must have put it there, how dare you! My husband is a Borough Councillor . . .*

So rather unwillingly, I tracked my quarry out of the train in his sheepskin. He proceeded with devilish cunning at a 2 mph amble with hawk-eye, in disguising spectacles, observing from the far side of the road. Chummy (see, it's coming) then entered a newsagent's. Suspecting a concealed exit, I followed and browsed ostentatiously by the stand, laying down my spectacles in an admirably natural manner, waiting until he paid and then brilliantly *leaving the shop first* loitering briefly outside . . .

Just as well I did loiter. Sheepskin hurried out looking for me, to return my glasses. I'm watching the house now (from a cafe, owing to not having a "parked van in which to lie on the floor covered by a blanket and holding a periscope against one of the side windows", or even a motorcycle sidecar with eye-holes cut in it). When he comes out again I shall glide through the streets in the old bungees; in a disguised gait and soft hat, tireless as a jungle hunter.

Or maybe I won't. I'm not sure I like it out there any more, what with all those sodden sock-thieves with their brollyfuls of nicked bacon, those huge-bloomered women, housebreakers' grannies, and trouser-dropping murderers who "seldom bury deep or carefully". No, there's this Bargain Pocket Calculator in the paper today. I might go home and send off for it.

"The job's off, fellas; the XJ12 Charlie's nicked for the getaway is worth more than the job itself."

"Excuse me, madam, but I have reason to suspect . . ."

A HONEYSETT QUARTET

"He's very disappointed he was found innocent."

"And I say it's the bloke in the middle."

"You got her to talk—now get her to shut up."

Red Herrings

According to *The Times,* the Chinese Communist press has denounced Agatha Christie as "a running-dog for the rich and powerful. She described crimes committed by the lower classes of British society, but never explained their social causes". True, true, replies ALAN COREN, which is probably why the Chinese always produced their own versions . . .

From LORD LICKSPITTLE DIES

"Alors," said Hercule Poirot, when the three hundred and eighty servants gathered in the library had finished touching their forelocks, "you are probably wondering why I have asked you all here *ce soir.*"

"Is it to have our faces ground again, master?" enquired an under-gardener, his huge peasant frame with its magnificent muscles forged by long years of service with the effete Lickspittle cringing now, as was required of all those who wished their little ones to eat.

"*Comment?*" said the rotund bourgeois parasite.

"We normally have our faces ground every Thursday after dinner," explained the strapping worker, "but as Lord Lickspittle was murdered this morning, we thought the grinding might have been brought forward to fit in with the funeral arrangements."

"*Non, non, non!*" snapped the agent provacateur, in that same imperialist tongue used to lash the heroes of Indo-China in the days before the glorious people's revolution swept their fascist oppressors from their land. "You are here because I have concluded that one of you is *l'assassin!* One of you battered that elegant *corps* to a bloody pulp and then removed its noble *tête* with a single savage *coup!*"

The crowd of pitiful slaves moaned and shook their sturdy heads and beat their toilworn breasts. Some of the tinier chimney boys sobbed openly, the hot tears coursing pale tracks down their blackened and emaciated faces.

"How could that be, master?" cried a wizened cat-groom, his fear of the whip overcome by his need to speak up. "Did we not love the mighty Lord Lickspittle, who never failed to fill our daily trough with nourishing gruel?"

"He always gave us a half-day off at Christmas!" chimed in a valiant cue-chalker.

"He always gave us a new shiny threepenny bit when he got us pregnant!" called a lovely fresh-faced daughter of the soil, cupping her chapped and swollen hands to her mouth, the better to make her point.

"One of *vous* did not feel that way!" barked the vile Belgian collaborator. "That person took a blunt instrument and beat the unfortunate Lord Lickspittle to *mort.* And," he added, lowering his voice, "that same person then removed his *tête!*" He raised his voice again, wagging a fat finger at the crowd. "Now, *pourquoi,* I ask myself, would someone cut off the head of a victim who was already dead? Why would he run the *risque* of having to dispose of not just *un* weapon, but *deux?*" Poirot smiled a cruel smile. "It was not until I discovered both murder weapons that I realised the answer!"

And here, as the enslaved multitude gaped, the little pawn reached behind him and took something from a table.

"This hammer," he cried, "was used to batter *milord* lifeless!"

The crowd gasped! He reached again!

"*Et* this sickle," he screamed, the white foam flecking his red podgy lips, "was used to cut off his aristocratic *tête!*"

He held the glorious peoples' symbol aloft. The crowd fell back, rapt!

"From this I conclude," he screamed, "that the murder was a political act carried out by the one *homme* on this estate well-versed in the use of both implements, in other *mots,* Third Gardener With Special Responsibilities For Scything And Staking . . . Jasper Rumbelow!"

But instead of the crowd turning upon the miserable accused, a thousand years of capitalist exploitation and repression turned suddenly in upon itself! The seven hundred and sixty eyes did not for a second leave the upraised hammer and sickle shining in the revolting chandelier-light! A new gleam had come into those downtrodden eyes! Then, of a sudden,

"DEATH TO THE RUNNING DOGS OF YANKEE IMPERIALISM!" howled the heroic mob. "CHAIRMAN MAO WILL LIVE FOR A THOUSAND YEARS! LET THE HEROIC PEOPLES ANNIHILATE THE FAWNING HYENAS OF WALL STREET!"

And, in one glorious democratic surge, the crowd rose as one man and thrust forward over their gibbering enemy, treading his loathsome body into the carpet where it, with its awful secret, died!

From MURDER ON THE ORIENT BICYCLE

"What put me on the wrong track at the start," said Miss Marple, guzzling her tea in a manner which made it all too clear that she had never given a thought to the countless thousands who had worked their enslaved fingers to the bone, toiling away on sunbacked hillsides to pluck the leaves which would make their corrupt absentee landlords rich, nor to those who had struggled beneath the heel of their Imperial Pekinese tyrants to make porcelain delicate enough to suit the decadent tastes of the Western jackals lolling the afternoons away with their titled mistresses, "was that I was sure the murderer of Sir Winston Orient would be drawn from the ranks of those who stood to benefit from his will."

"A fair assumption," nodded Chief Inspector Hitler, "the Orient Bicycle Company was worth every penny of twenty million, gorblimey."

O foolish investigators! O blinkered fascists! Has your own overwhelming greed made you blind to the fact that man may have other motives beside profit? Has not the immortal Chairman Mao written: *I pluck a flower. You pluck a flower. We have two flowers. What need have we of a third flower?* If Sir Winston Orient had read that, might he not now be alive, instead of a permanent part of the Great West Road?

"Yes," said Miss Marple, nibbling a ginger nut with perfect dentures beyond the reach of England's gummy jobless, "but when Gerald Orient, Lady Emmeline Orient, Nigel Orient, Daisy ffoskett-Orient, and even little Webster Orient all died similar deaths, leaving no beneficiaries alive, financial gain could clearly not have been behind the holocaust."

"Quite," said the uniformed capitalist tool.

"Further," continued Miss Marple, in a cut-glass accent paid for by the sweat of millions, "I could not understand how it was that these people, who had been familiar with all manner of bicycles for over a century, could have all fallen from brand-new Orient machines at *exactly the same spot,* where the drive of Orient Hall meets the Great West Road, there to be ridden over by the terrible traffic. How did it come about that these bicycles went out of control at the bottom of the slope, turning themselves into murder weapons?"

"You got me beat, and no mistake," replied Hitler, who was as stupid as he was powerful, a characteristic of Ireland Yard's neo-Gestapo hierarchy.

"So I approached the conundrum from a different direction," the hag went on, "and worked out exactly who *would* benefit from the deaths of all the Orients. It took four weeks for the obvious answer to reveal itself to me, Chief Inspector!"

"Four weeks, knock me down with a feather?" replied Hitler.

"Four weeks during which the fortunes of The Orient Bicycle Company went steadily down. It was, despite its immense size, still a family-run business, you see; and with the deaths of the entire Board, the thing just fell into disorder."

"Bound to," interrupted the class-traitor, "with the bosses gone."

Idiot jackal! Is it any wonder the solution eludes you yet, ignorant as you are of the world of the heroic worker? Can you not see how capitalism is careful to leave only chaos behind it, to fake bogus proof of its desirability?

"Quite," continued Miss Marple. "But at the end of those disastrous weeks, what did the Government do but step in with funds and—here is the important part, Chief Inspector—*turn the factories over to the control of their workers!* Now that you see who benefits, does the identity of the murderer not become crystal-clear?"

"A worker!" shrieked Hitler.

She shook her horrible head.

"Not *a* worker," she replied, "*all* the workers! It was a conspiracy."

How the guile of the lying West may twist the wondrous concept of solidarity to suit its own nefarious purposes, my comrades!

"They all did something to the bicycles, then?"

"Correct. But exactly what it was, I did not realise until I noticed again a piece of graffiti in one of the lavatories whose import I had ignored before. On the wall was written DIE PROLETARIER HABEN NICHTS IN IHR ZU VERLIEREN ALS IHRE KETTEN."

"I know that quotation!" exclaimed the oaf. "It is from the original edition of Marx's *Communist Manifesto*! I have beaten it out of long-haired poofter drug-addicts on many an occasion. It means THE WORKERS HAVE NOTHING TO LOSE BUT THEIR CHAINS." He paused. His vile face lit up. "Of course! They removed the chains! At the bottom of the slope, the Orients suddenly discovered . . . "

"Not quite, Chief Inspector. I'm afraid the German infiltrator had taken the British worker to be rather better educated than he is, ha-ha-ha!"

Thus do the moribund upper classes sneer at their true superiors! Is their imminent doom not justly deserved?

"I don't understand," said the police butcher.

"Nor did I until I asked someone, in a casual manner, to translate it for me. 'Everybody knows that,' he replied, 'it means THE WORKERS HAVE NOTHING TO LOSE BUT THEIR CATS.' Then he turned pale and ran off, and I saw it all."

"I don't," answered the dolt.

"It's very simple. Once I knew that the workers were prepared to sacrifice their cats to serve their revolutionary ends, I examined the murder spot again. And what do you suppose I found, buried beneath

the hedge that flanks the gates of Orient Hall?"
"What?"
"Six dead cats, each with the marks of a brand-new Orient bicycle tyre across it!" exclaimed the prying scourge of oppressed millions everywhere. "There had been nothing wrong with the bicycles themselves! But as each had sped down that hill, a murderous worker crouching behind the gate had flung his cat in its path! The startled Orients had hit the cats, gone out of control, swerved into the road, and been flattened by lorries!"

The police pig fell back astonished.

"But—but we can't arrest the entire factory!" he stammered.

"No," nodded the spy. She closed her file. "I do not think there is anything we can do. There were just too many of them."

And for once the old witch was right, comrades! Solidarity had triumphed! The people's democratic will had conquered all in its path! It was a very great day indeed!

"Another thing—the auditors are querying your expenses claim for the journey to Parkhurst."

The Case of the Law v. Justice

FENTON BRESLER and MAHOOD adjudicate

NOW is not a happy time for British justice. Sir Peter Rawlinson, Chairman of the Bar, may well proclaim with all his customary mellifluousness at the recent Annual Conference of the Law Society: "Judged by the standards and experience of other free societies the administration of justice in this country is outstanding." But that is hardly to impose an impossibly high criterion. I have no doubt that British justice still is, in the cant phrase, "the best in the world"—but is that saying all that much?

What is disquieting is that we are falling down on our own standards. It was never true to say, as the late Mr Justice Humphreys once did with all the arrogance of one-time judicial complacency, "a miscarriage of justice in the country is as rare as a black tulip." But in recent years the increasing inadequacy of the law even to approximate to justice has become one of the few growth-industries that has really been booming.

In bygone days, the idea of a Bill of Rights, a written code of the essential personal rights of a British citizen that no Parliament nor judge could take away, was regarded as anathema to the whole ethos of our law. Inadequate foreigners, such as the Americans or West Germans, may have needed such a prop to liberty. But in Britain? Never. Perish the thought.

As far back as 1610, Sir Edward Coke was declaring with all the sonority that for centuries characterised the utterances of our senior judges, "The Common Law will control Acts of Parliament and sometimes adjudge them to be utterly void." And in another case he trumpeted with utter confidence that the words of an Act of Parliament "Shall not bind the King's Bench . . . "

Now their Lordships speak with muted tongue. It takes one of the most gifted of current judges, Lord Justice Scarman, in his 1974 Hamlyn Lectures to pronounce the unpalatable truth: "The Common Law is no longer the strong, independent ally but the servant of Parliament . . .

"I'm undecided whether to give you a long sentence and teach you a lesson or let you loose on society and teach them a lesson!"

Without a Bill of Rights, protected from repeal, amendment or suspension by the ordinary processes of a bare Parliamentary majority controlled by the government of the day, human rights will be at risk." Nor is he alone. Lord Hailsham, Lord Salmon, Lord Shawcross, the Liberal Party, the National Council for Civil Liberties, Sir Keith Joseph—these somewhat ill-assorted bedfellows all believe that Britain's legal ills can be cured by a piece of paper.

So far only Professor Harry Street of Manchester University has made the obvious point—also in a speech at the Law Society's last Annual Conference—that the Bill of Rights will still have to be interpreted and enforced by the judges; and "considering all the occasions in the past when the courts have had the opportunity to protect the citizen by adapting the Common Law, and have failed to rule against the Executive, how sure can we be that the courts will welcome the task of declaring a law which Parliament has passed to be void because it was inconsistent with the Bill of Rights?"

It was Lord Parker, the late Lord Chief Justice, who once described the judiciary in an unguarded moment as "the hand-maiden of the Executive"; and he trailed more than his petticoat when he admitted in a 1964 House of Lords debate, "I think that today self-preservation against criticism would make (the judges) progressive." One shudders at what is meant by "progressive" in this context.

The bravery of the judges, of course, is not in question. Courageous in their personal lives, they certainly are. I have left the Old Bailey at the end of a day's sitting and driven away in his car with an elderly judge presiding over a terrorist trial completely unprotected by the police and without a plain-clothes man in sight.

No one tells a judge what to do. I am sure of that. Judicial independence, in the sense of freedom from official or State direction, is as real as it has ever been—possibly more so. The modern judge has long since ceased to be a political appointment. They are no one's straw men.

Yet one senses a creeping demoralisation, a sort of ever-thickening smoke-screen of lack of confidence in their position and their authority bellowing out over the trenches of the battlefield between the law and its denigrators.

Last month, Mr Justice Mais directed that a man who had pleaded guilty, through diminished responsibility, to the manslaughter of his wife because of his morbid psychotic jealousy, should be treated at Glenside mental hospital. In accordance with the relevant provisions of the 1959 Mental Health Act, the judge only made the order after the consent of the hospital and the doctor who would be treating him there had been obtained. But the staff's shop stewards' committee did not agree. They threatened "industrial action" if the court's order was implemented and the man admitted for treatment.

So what happened? Did Mr Justice Mais threaten the shop stewards with imprisonment for contempt of court? That would be naive to expect. "I have no alternative," he said, "but to deliver a sentence which I consider to be wholly inadequate"—and he varied the man's sentence to life imprisonment. Terrence Shaw, the *Daily Telegraph's* Legal Correspondent, commented that the learned Judge had thereby "defused the situation", as if that were matter for congratulation.

I could not help thinking back to May 1974 when Mr Justice Donaldson, by accepting at the last moment payment by a mysterious "anonymous group of industrialists" of the £65,000 debt owed by Hugh Scanlon's engineering union to the Industrial Relations Court, saved the economy from a ruinous 24 hours' nation-wide protest strike. He

*"Face facts, man—you're an under-priviliged black radical left-wing unemployed person of no fixed address with an Irish accent—**of course you're guilty!**"*

stressed that acceptance in no way purged the union's contempt—but ignored the question of any penalty being imposed for it. "We are delighted that the situation should be defused, provided it does not involve the surrender of some of the authority of the court," said the resolute Sir John Donaldson.

Nowadays, Her Majesty's Judges tend to sound more like electricians than upholders of the law. What business is it of theirs to "defuse" the situation between law-enforcers and law-breakers? What is wrong with a little honest confrontation?

Life has a habit of making the cap fit. Down-grading one's own status brings its own reward. Earlier this year, Mr Justice Willis sentenced a man to ten years in gaol; and promptly advised him to appeal. He said he wanted to make a hospital order against the man who admitted a serious sexual offence against a 12-year-old boy. But the Government department concerned had declined to inform him whether there was a vacancy in a top security mental hospital. He therefore had to impose a gaol sentence. "Perhaps the Court of Appeal will be treated with more courtesy by the Government department than I have been," the judge said plaintively.

One sometimes feels like saying, "Judge Jeffreys, thou shouldst be living at this hour. England has need of thee." Did anyone else notice that on the same day that a bomb blew up underneath Hugh Fraser's car killing one of the most eminent cancer research specialists of the day, the Court of Appeal cut the sentences imposed on four I.R.A. sympathisers for their part in earlier Manchester bomb outrages because "sentences imposed for bombs primarily intended to destroy property should be significantly less than those designed

"You are sentenced to twenty years in prison but as this court wishes to show mercy you will be excused visits from Lord Longford."

to put life at risk?" A bomb is a bomb, one would have thought.

Look what happens when a judge *does* speak his mind, and says something which is against the grain of "progressive" thought. In May of this year, Judge Gwynn Morris had a case before him at the Old Bailey where five West Indian youths from Brixton were convicted of several vicious robberies upon unaccompanied women in the street. "These attacks have become a monotonous feature in the suburbs of Brixton and Clapham, areas which within living memory were peaceful, safe and agreeable to live in," said the judge.

"But the immigrant resettlement which has occurred over the past twenty-five years has radically transformed that environment.

"Those concerned with the maintenance of law and order are confronted with immense difficulties. This case has highlighted and underlined the perils which confront honest, innocent and hardworking women who are in the street after nightfall.

"I notice that not a single West Indian woman was attacked. The court's duty is to protect the public.

"In doing so, I pray that parents will do what they can to impose discipline among the young. Failure to do so will lead inevitably to massive social disorder."

"Six ruddy medical experts and they can't even agree on whether the ***judge*** *is sane!"*

I must confess that I can see nothing wrong in those remarks. They were a comment upon the state of the law in South-West London that was totally within the competence of the judge to give, and temperately expressed. Yet the furore! The inevitable snide article upon "the wit and wisdom of Judge Morris" from the *Sunday Times,* protests from Colonel Marcus Lipton, the local, far from publicity-shy M.P., David Stephen of the Runnymede Trust, Mark Bonham Carter of the Community Relations Commission, *et al.* Is it any wonder most judges keep their heads down, their mouths shut—and their sentences low?

"We are becoming cynical and bitter," Sergeant Leslie Male, Chairman of the Police Federation, told a Federation delegate meeting two months ago, "when our work in bringing offenders to justice is nearly always made worthless by the courts who, by their failure to impose adequate and sensible punishments are, in fact, encouraging the law-breaker and slapping the honest citizen in the face." Reform cannot come at grass roots level. It must come from on high—from the judges themselves. Police frustration shows itself in many different ways. Why, for instance, was Young Liberals leader and prominent anti-apartheid demonstrator Peter Hain kept in solitary confinement for twelve hours before being charged recently with that improbable offence of stealing £490 from a nearby bank and only then finally allowed home? Why was the identity parade held two days *after* he was charged?

Why, on a different plane, do the police harass motorists and seem only too keen to institute prosecutions against normally law-abiding citizens for apparent trivia—while strangely reluctant to intervene when squatters unlawfully take over other people's homes or protesting Channel ferry-men impound innocent passengers' cars and prevent them driving their own property ashore? Could it be because intervention in socially "delicate" areas leads to hassle and problems—but the ordinary chap is anybody's fall-guy?

The police are only human. They do not work in a vacuum. They operate within a framework laid down by the judges. And if they are beginning to feel that their particular game is not worth the candle, that influential voices are against them, that even if they get their man before the court he will only be let off with a sermon and a prayer, who honestly can blame them?

Recently, a 15-year-old boy appeared before a juvenile court with a batch of previous convictions to his name. "These kids would not have such a bad record if the police would not keep arresting them," a social worker told the magistrates. That about sums up the state of justice and the law today.

A Simple Glossary of Legal Terms

MILES KINGTON

Appeal: Legal version of double or quits.

As your Lordship well remembers: Hint by a barrister that he is about to refer to a completely forgotten and, possibly, imaginary case.

Bail: A surety so large that it may even exceed a lawyer's fees. Many lawyers are said to fall down and worship bail.

Barrister: One who agrees to commit perjury in return for money. One who speaks the language of the law (see Law). At this very moment, 50% of all working barristers are engaged in committing perjury in legal language; to do them credit, they lead otherwise quite normal lives and do not let it weigh on their conscience for a minute.

Bresler: One who seeks to turn legal language into English in return for money.

Capital Punishment: The system of killing a criminal to ensure that he does not repeat his crime. The pros and cons have been so often argued that there is nothing left to say about it, except the little-known, conversation-stopping fact that the first European country to ban it was Liechtenstein (1798).

Conspiracy: When the authorities feel sure that someone has done something wrong but are not sure what, they arrest him on a charge of conspiracy. It is the legal embodiment of the English dislike of people who are too clever for their own good.

Costs: The amount of money needed to bankrupt an acquitted person.

Criminal Law: One that no government in its right mind should ever have passed.

Damages: What is left over after the lawyers and the courts have taken their share.

Edgar Lustgarten: One who dramatises legal language in return for money; one who has noticed that lawyers' statements are not copyright.

Fine: If a defendant is adjudged to have made money by illegal methods, he is often punished by being fined, that is, by being forced to watch the state enjoy his ill-gotten gains.

GBH. George Bernard haw. A misprint.

Hung Jury: In the bad old Victorian days, the jury was occasionally taken forth and hanged if it could not agree.

In Camera: Private showing of pornographic films.

Jury: Cornerstone of British justice; the right of any shifty, half-witted, scheming villain to be judged by his peers.

Law: The language spoken by lawyers. Also, the attempt by Parliament to define the difference between right and wrong, a question which has stumped the greatest philosophers of all time.

Letter of the Law: A document written on thick vellum, with illustrated initial letters, wrapped in best pink ribbon and costing sums of money beyond the Post Office's wildest dreams.

Legal Aid: If a barrister is too poor to get his own cases, the state will provide them for him free of charge.

Libel: An uncomfortable home truth, which it is fortunately illegal to publish.

Mackenzie's friend: An unpaid legal adviser, and therefore an abhorrence to the law. Also, a Scottish homosexual.

Non volenti fit injuria: No legal glossary would be complete without at least one Latin phrase. This one means: "No-one in the aircraft was hurt."

Oath: Method of allying perjury to blasphemy.

Precedent: A trick which has been tried before, successfully.

Queen's Proctor: An officer of the law whose job is to prevent young gentlemen climbing over the walls of Buckingham Palace after mid-night.

Res ipsa loquitur: Another Latin phrase, for good measure. It means: "The thing speaks for itself." Anything that speaks for itself is an abomination in the sight of the law. It should pay a lawyer to speak for it.

Respect, With: Hint that a barrister is about to be disrespectful.

Signed, Sealed and Delivered: An example of lawyers being paid threefold for what is only one job. We may be sure that it was a lawyer who devised hanging, drawing and quartering.

Slander: A kind of character assassination which is forbidden among the general public but much enjoyed by judges when giving judgement.

Solicitor: One who panders for business, e.g. one who writes to a celebrity and points out that he may have been libelled in a recent article in *Punch* and with luck they may get a few quid out of court.

Sub judice: A method of restricting comment on a matter of public interest until it is too late.

Subject to Contract: A legal admission that an Englishman's word is anything but his bond.

Taking silk: Much like taking lead or copper but not half so cumbersome.

Tort: See "Puddy tat."

Under Appeal: Second helpings of sub judice.

Vix causa, vix necessitas: Latin phrase meaning that having a good reason to do something is not necessarily good enough in law. It has never been used in English law, for the simple reason that we have just made it up. How many lawyers among our readers spotted that?

Wherefore: Meaningless word used by solicitors to introduce other meaningless words.

Xanadu: Place where Kubla Khan decreed a stately pleasure dome. That was before he applied for planning permission, of course.

Yes, My Lord: Witty rejoinder by barrister to judge.

Zub Judice: Restricted comment during West Country trial.

THERE'S NO BUSINESS LIKE FUNNY BUSINESS

According to a cost-benefit study of underworld profitability, crime runs I.C.I. close in the industry profits league. MAHOOD looks at how the criminal fraternity is adapting to the big business life

"According to McKinsey you're indulging in too much smash and not enough grab!"

"The penalty of success, I'm afraid—it's a takeover bid!"

"We're hoping to attract more graduates into the business, particularly those who cheated in their exams."

"Any chance of two hundred stick-up and one hundred ransom notes by five, Rosie?"

"No, no Louie! Write him a memo."

"Hold it, boys—he's forgotten his gold watch!"

The Trouble with Real Life

BASIL BOOTHROYD

"Store detective Mrs Theresa Kiteley burst into tears last night."

Daily Mail

WELL, it was awful. She'd arrested an innocent man, got in a mess with her statements, had her case thrown out of court and been told off by Judge Peter Solomon in forthright terms, even for a man rendered testy, perhaps, by a lifetime of Old Testament jokes about dividing babies in half.

It all reminded me of what is often regarded as Sir A. Conan Doyle's most moving passage:

As I rushed into the room he raised streaming eyes from his roughly bandaged knee.

"Holmes!" I cried. "That villain has shot you! Say you have brought him to justice!"

"It was no villain, Watson," blubbed he, "but a harmless grocer from Hoxton. And I clumsily shot myself."*

Dr. Watson, you'll remember, then threw himself down beside the dear, aquiline legs, noticing almost at once that his friend had bandaged the wrong one.

Taking another example, did you catch the recent *Cannon* screening, where he tailed a suspect into a drugstore, was made the subject of a citizen's arrest by the soda-jerk, and is now doing five to ten in the State pen, a Quinn Martin Production?

If not, and back to women dicks, you may have seen police sergeant Angie Dickinson the other night. She was posing as an air hostess, in a dope case and a daftly designed uniform hat even for air hostesses, and the baddies got clean away after pushing her off a tall building, if I remember aright.

Perhaps I don't.

It's a far cry from the Wood Green branch of Woolworth's, where ex-police-woman Mrs Kiteley, subsequently a store detective for fifteen years, thought she'd spotted a customer nicking a small tin of tyre-black, to the home of Senator George McGovern, in East Hampton, NY.

* *Wetness for the Prosecution* (from *The Misadventures*)

Luckily I'm in good voice today, and can carry the distance with ease.

You may need a bit of help, though. Senator McGovern, according to the Beeb's overseas service—which disconcertingly ends its bulletins, "And that is the End of the World News", no part of my argument, but I've been wanting to mention it for some time—George McGovern, it seems has recently come into possession of information showing that the CIA, while the States were having their Hate Cuban Cigars period, made "over forty unsuccessful attempts" to assassinate Fidel Castro.

I don't know whether I should repeat that, just to drive the figure home. Over forty, it was. In excess of two score. If it sticks better, call it XL-plus.

This strikes me as a lot, and while you're coming round to my view of it you may care to ask, meanwhile, (a) what tyre-black is, and (b), how did the anti-Castro push turn out?

With (b) I can assist. Have, indeed, done so. Didn't I use the word unsuccessful? It turned out fine, anyway for Castro, who is alive and well and living in hopes of many more three-hour TV talks. In just the same situation, in fact, give or take a few obvious distinctions, as Mrs. Kiteley's late prisoner, the man from Merstham who is rightly walking around free without a stain on his whitewalls, having been awarded costs from public funds and custody of the small, mysterious tin.

These aren't things that happen to anyone Theo Kojak gets after, to say nothing of Harry O, Banacek, Colombo, Steve McGarret, Perry (now Ironside) Mason, old squash-nose Thingummy who used to dress up as more parsons than Bing Crosby but now cleans up the Streets of San Francisco, McCloud, Barnaby Jones, Chief Macmillan, *et al,* and let's throw in Father Brown for older readers.

Nor do the enemies of America, dedicated as it is to the unalienable rights of life, liberty and the pursuit of Commies, with any frequency elude all those thinly disguised CIA operatives whom we may class for present purposes as the Men from Uncle, who occupy numberless miles of Hollywood videotape, and who would have done Castro in a single 50-min. instalment even if he'd been time-locked in a concrete bathyscaphe at the bottom of Havana harbour and encircled by booby-trapped whales.

It was Edward G. Robinson, an insurance sleuth in a big-armholed waistcoat at the time, who fired off that memorable speech in *Double Indemnity,* listing the accepted ways of taking life. It seemed pretty comprehensive, but I don't think he rattled off more than a dozen, with punctuating cigar jabs. I admit that this was before our own more enlightened times, when most door knobs are wired for 10,000 volts, alarm clocks constantly trigger 7·56 Mausers, and no one can turn an ignition key without getting his tattered remains blown through the nearest plate glass window.

Even so, I still take the view, and hope you've come round to it after that bit of pondering time I've given you, that forty attempts to finalise Fidel is excessive. We're talking, after all, about specialists. Those CIA boys aren't stu—. Well, they know their stuff. And you can bet that each attempt was different. Any average Head of State, once he's seen his hired food-taster turn green and dead with a soup spoon on his lips, or found his underpants poisoned, or gelignite in the air-conditioning, will be on his guard against specific recurrences. Oh, no, they'd have had to keep dreaming up fresh ideas, though we laymen, denied access to the Agency training manual, may find it hard to conceive how they dreamed up more than forty.

More than forty.

It's even harder to conceive how the whole damned lot flopped. I've forgotten who the boss was at the time, and I expect he'll be glad that someone has. He's had his irritations already, if you ask me, as the boys kept reporting back from mission after mission, twenty, twenty-five, thirty, thirty-five . . . and not one of them with so much as Castro's hat to throw down on the desk. Get even one failure like that from a TV writer, and he's trying to get additional-dialogue work in *The Wonderful World of Disney*.

This, I fear, is the Grand Discrepancy. Between grainy old fact and appetising fiction. It has teased us all, since immemorial time, from the Greeks, fooled by old Athenian scriptmen into thinking the gods were running things and finding it was just the Colonels, through Piers Plowman fans, lured into farm work in the expectation of meeting people crying 'Hot pies, hot!' all over the place, right up to those gullible followers of the telly-fuzz in its infinite variety, who now face bitter disillusionment in the shape of Mrs. T. Kiteley, the weeping detective of hopeless incompetence who, as if she hadn't suffered enough, stigmatised as a girl who can't even keep her private eye on a tin of tyre-black without losing the scent—if it has a scent, I've no information on that—has also received rather less coverage in these columns than I'd originally intended.

Too bad, and I'm sorry. But don't give up, Mrs. K., is my concluding message. Damn it, you've only failed once. Think of the CIA.

Even if you keep on failing, it doesn't mean your career is over. To judge from the revealed facts, about both your goodself and the Agency boys, you could be just the girl they're looking for.

One of our Spies is Miss Inge

KEITH WATERHOUSE'S classic tale of treachery, passion, espionage and suspense in Wimbledon

Half a million civil servants have been warned to watch out for a new security risk. Beware the au pair girl from a Communist country, they are told in a memorandum. She could be a potential spy in your home.—*Daily Mail* report.

MR. WHITSUN BANK-HOLIDAY, for the Prosecution, said that this was a shocking case. It was a case of a so-called au pair girl—the accused, Olga Karamazova—coming to these shores, inveigling herself into the employ of a decent English household, and repaying their hospitality by embarking upon a career of espionage.

Mr. Whitsun Bank-Holiday said that he would be as brief as possible. Mr. T. Drinker was a senior civil servant at the Ministry of Defence, with special responsibility towards the survival of the Queen's subjects in the event of a nuclear attack. Mrs. Drinker was a keen gardener and a member of the Wimbledon Cheery Folks, an amateur concert party. There were two children of the marriage—Kevin and Barbara, aged five and seven respectively.

The court would hear that until November 1970 the Drinker family's au pair girl was one Netochka Nezvanova, from Portugal. Senorita Nezvanova had been diligent in her work and indeed satisfactory in every way. She was a keen "ham" radio enthusiast and often allowed the children to play with her Morse tapper. It was only when some men came to fetch her in a big black car that her period of employment was reluctantly terminated.

What more natural than that the Drinker family should go to the Vladimir Lenin Domestic Agency and Institute of Cultural Research, the same agency which had supplied Senorita Nezvanova, to find a replacement?

It was no part of the prosecution's task to question the integrity of the Vladimir Lenin Domestic Agency. It was a reputable firm which had occupied the same registered offices—the second bench along as you went round Kensington Pond in a clockwise direction—since 1958. Having shown Mr. Drinker a microfilm copy of Olga Karamazova's references in good faith the Agency's obligations were discharged. Mr Drinker duly deposited the Agency's fee in a hollow oak tree near the Albert Memorial, and the accused subsequently left her home in Switzerland and joined the Drinker household later that same week.

Mrs. Drinker would tell the court that Olga Karamazova appeared to settle down happily enough in the Wimbledon menage, and that every effort was made to accommodate her. A keen amateur photographer and homing-pigeon enthusiast, she was readily given permission to convert the cupboard under the stairs into a darkroom, and the attic into a pigeon loft. She was interested in the radio equipment that Senorita Nezvanova had left behind, and was allowed to borrow it. Having joined a social club—the Central Committee for Au Pair Girls in Exile—she was rarely denied an afternoon off to attend its meetings. She was, despite her eccentric habit of eating slips of paper with writing on them, encouraged to take her meals with the family.

It would be for the jury to decide whether, in view of subsequent events, Olga Karamazova might be said to have bitten the hand that fed her. Whether she arrived at the Drinker establishment from Switzerland with the deliberate, preconceived intention of spying, or whether she later succumbed to temptation, was neither here nor there.

Mrs. Drinker would swear on oath that in June of this year the affairs of the Cheery Folks concert party bore heavily on her mind. She had undertaken to write, produce and appear in a sketch tentatively entitled, "At the Dentist's." During this same month Mr. Drinker was greatly occupied with a master-plan of all the deep air raid shelters in Britain which he was preparing for his masters at the Ministry of Defence. Mr. Drinker was obliged to bring work home at weekends. Mrs. Drinker had her gardening activities as well as the Cheery Folks. It fell to Olga Karamazova, during this hectic period, to take sole charge of the children, Kevin and Barbara.

Both the Drinkers would agree in evidence that at first they had no grounds for complaint. Karamazova, like any Swiss girl new to London, was interested in the tourist attractions of the city, and she seemed eager and willing to take the children on a series of outings to such places as London Docks, Trafalgar Square, RAF Station Uxbridge, the basement of the War Office and so on and so forth.

However, the jury would learn from Mr. Drinker that at about this time Olga Karamazova began to take an interest in his briefcase. She was always present in the morning to hand it to him as he left for the Ministry; always there in the evening to relieve him of it when he arrived home. On several occasions, according to Mr. Drinker, she said that the briefcase was in a shabby condition and offered to take it down to her dark-room to give it a good polish. It would be for the jury to decide whether the accused took an unusual interest in Mr. Drinker's briefcase.

Mr. Whitsun Bank-Holiday said that on the fourth of July, Olga Karamazova had charge of the children for the entire day. Barbara and Kevin were too young to appear in the witness box, but they had made depositions, and in those sworn depositions, they had said, in part, as follows: "Nana came to our room at approximately 8.23 am. She said to us, 'And zees morning, we go to zee secret missile base, no? Barbara will carry zee binoculars, Kevin zee camera, and I zee sandwiches.' We agreed to this plan."

Witness after witness would prove that Olga Karamazova took the children nowhere near the secret missile base that day. She led them, instead, to the Ministry of Defence, on the thin pretext that, having forgotten a dolly belonging to the child Barbara, she would have to borrow Mr. Drinker's key and return to Wimbledon.

The commissionaire would say that Karamazova arrived during Mr. Drinker's lunch-hour. That she knew full well it was Mr. Drinker's lunch-hour would be proved in due course. She was escorted to Mr. Drinker's office where his briefcase lay on the desk. That Karamazova seized the briefcase and then hurried the children down the fire-escape would also be proved to the hilt.

Karamazova, the jury would hear, was arrested in Green Park shortly after she had handed the briefcase to a Swiss compatriot named Ivan Dostoievsky. Dostoievsky, unfortunately, had been able to make his escape to Zurich, with the briefcase.

Mr. Whitsun Bank-Holiday, in conclusion, said that no doubt the jury would be curious to know what that briefcase contained. It contained, as the accused must have well known, a complete draft of the sketch, "At the Dentist's" which Mrs. Drinker had written for the Cheery Folks concert party, and which Mr. Drinker habitually carried with him in order to study the leading role, that of Dr. I. Pullem.

Thanks to Olga Karamazova's duplicity, thanks to her ingratitude, thanks to her treachery, that sketch was now in the hands of a foreign power. No doubt it was only a matter of time before a pirated version of it appeared on Swiss television. As for British concert parties—an institution which every decent Englishman held dear—their activities had been set back by at least twelve months. It was a grave charge upon which Olga Karamazova stood indicted and one which, if the jury agreed that the case was proved, deserved to be visited with the full rigour of the law.

"Mine are at a terrorist training camp. Keeps them out of mischief."

Unsafe as Houses

STANLEY REYNOLDS enters a few outrageous premises

YOU know how it is, you are standing there in the bus queue waiting for the number 11 or the 82 or the 54 and it is so boring and there is always some wag who says something like "They ought to call this the banana service. Because it comes in bunches. Get it? Ha ha!" So to brighten up the conversation you say, "Looks like rain, eh?" And the next thing you start worrying out loud.

"Gee," you say, "I got a Tintoretto hanging right alongside the living room window and I think I forgot to close it. The Giotto of course is on the other side of the room and the rain won't get it. And what the hell! All the Cezannes, Renoirs, Pissarros and Monets are early stuff. Let 'em get rained on. But all this damp weather has played hell on the silver filigree, a delicate tracery of fine silver ornamental work, which surrounds the wife's emeralds. They're the Krishnamurthy Emeralds, y'know. Used to belong to the Maharaja of Vizianagram's great uncle who gave them to the wife's granny on a tiger shoot in '97. He said she was his little chickadee and fleet-footed gazelle. They do it on the back of elephants out there, y'know. Shoot tigers that is. The wife's still got a marvellous collection of skins. They'd fetch a fortune at Sotheby's, a fellow said."

This, I have now learned, is a big mistake. And I hadn't even mentioned the Van Eyck gathering dust in the loft. I should have stuck to falling about at this fellow's joke about the buses being a banana service because although he may look like George something or other who lives down the road in a house called L'Abri and goes in for topiary, attempting to get his shrubs into ornamental peacock shapes but only ever succeeding in making them look like a couple of dogs in need of a swill down with a bucket of cold water, he may be a complete stranger disguised as George the amateur and inept topiarian. In short, he could be a burglar.

I had, I must confess, been rather simple-minded about this threat until the other day when a leaflet entitled *Protect Your Home,* prepared, it said, for the Home Office by the Central Office of Information, came through my letter slot. Accustomed chiefly as I am to the garish red-inked notices of the telephone people and folk who supply the electricity giving me seven days to cough up or else, I fell upon this new reading matter without the slightest notion that paranoia lurked within. On the first page was a four-colour photograph of what looked like my teenage son's bedroom. Clothes were strewn about the floor, the bureau drawers half opened with other garments protruding in a messy fashion. Upon closer inspection I saw that the Frank Zappa and Steely Dan posters had been taken from the walls. This was a photo of my teenage son's room after some burglar for reasons best known to himself—and who really knows the criminal mind?—had broken in for the Frank Zappa posters.

Naturally I have almost always cancelled the milk deliveries and the newspapers and closed those windows that the catches still work on before heading off on a holiday to bask upon a silver sanded beach in case I return, like the fellow in the TV public service advert, to twenty-four pints of rancid milk, a fortnight's back copies of bad news, and a ransacked house. I've gone even further than that. I don't go on holiday. Not that I sit at home chewing my nails, cricket bat in hand and padded up, box and all, just in case a cat thief manages to scale the battlements of my semi-detached.

At least I never went to those lengths until I read this Home Office leaflet. There was one particularly edgy note, printed in red ink, which quotes some anonymous chap boasting "I've nothing worth stealing." Underneath this piece of inverted snobbery it warns that "we all have things of sentimental value, even if they're worth little in hard cash."

Having been reared on 'tec stories and old movies in which people were always saying something like "if he had not taken to a life of crime he might have been a top flight brain surgeon or president of the Woonsockett Rhode Island First National Bank and Trust," I have always had respect for the criminal brain. So why lift "things of sentimental value, even if they're worth little or nothing in hard cash?" Obviously the Home Office knows something we don't. There is, apparently, a gang of bandits going around stealing things of sentimental value just for the nasty kicks.

Anyway, I got over that and read through the usual scam about making sure the man who has come to cut your electricity off has an identity card and scrapes his feet on the door mat, and those rather mind-spinning illustrations showing the sort of door locks, chains, padlocks and window locks which the Home Office thinks desirable.

They even have a peep-hole like the ones in the old speak-easy gangster movies where you say, "Joe sent me," and then you walk in to a line of chorus girls in black stockings, top hats cocked saucily over one eye. The peep-hole is called a door viewer and the Home Office claims you can get one for as little as £1·15 and I am seriously thinking of sending away although don't expect too much more than the occasional blonde swinging on an enamelled steel dome lightshade once you get inside.

There is also a two-page spread entitled *Look After Your Car* which gives some useful tips such as always remove the ignition key and if you forget to lock your car don't leave granny's Krishnamurthy Emeralds lounging around on the back seat. "At a recent kerbside check," it says, "in six major cities, an average of one car in four was found to be insecure." This had me all right. Now these Home Office leaflets have, evidently, been getting pushed through letter slots all over Britain. And if Home Office statistics are correct criminals must be living on the other side of those letter slots. What is going to keep them from saying, when you discover one of them attempting to force an entrance into your Vauxhall Viva or 1925 3-Litre Bentley, "Sorry, fella, I'm Home Office, we're doing a kerbside check in six major cities."

He might even flash some bogus Home Office credentials at you, saying he is entitled to break into cars in six major cities. How am I supposed to know what these credentials are supposed to look like? At least when the electricity man shows up at the door he has the magic password. He says, "You owe £190·83, mate," and you know in your heart of hearts that he is the real thing.

But the item in *Protect Your Home* which really stirred the old paranoia came under a cosy looking photo of a bunch of chaps having a quiet pint in what looked like a decent looking pub, not too tarted up, and probably with a pint of Campaign for Real Ale approved bitter, on draught. But the caption told us: "Beware Strangers." Then there followed various warnings about chatting in pubs and bus queues etc, which would kill the art of conversation stone dead if not start a fashion for going out with masking tape sealing your lips.

As these things work out I tossed aside *Protect Your Home* and had only just started flipping my way through that day's *Daily Mirror* when my eye caught a letter from a Mr F. Reeves of New Mills, Derbyshire, who says he is "so disgusted by some misleading mail-order offers for articles from books to wine that I now refuse to read such correspondence." Mr Reeves perhaps got himself a plain brown envelope full of bad Algerian masquerading as Château-Pichon-Longueville through the post. It is a problem I for some reason do not have. Aside from the firm from whom

I purchased a complete set of double glazing who keep mailing me invitations to buy more double glazing (maybe they think the burglars have snatched the old ones) I am apparently, unlike the frazzled Mr Reeves, not on any mail-order house list. After reading *Protect Your Home,* however, maybe one of those mail-order firms could push a crate of man-eating Alsatians through my letter slot. On the other hand, if any strange crate does come through the post I might give it a short blast with the 12 bore. You never know, a stranger may be lurking inside, all ears.

"As the law assumes they are all innocent until proved guilty, I assume they are all guilty until proved innocent and that way we get an even balance."